William Shakespeare's HAMLET

Leonora Brodwin
Associate Professor of English
St. John's University

Laurie Rozakis, Ph.D.
The State University of New York
at Farmingdale

1997 Barnes & Noble Books

MACMILLAN is a registered trademark of Macmillan, Inc.
Monarch and colophons are trademarks of Simon & Schuster, Inc.,
registered in the U.S. Patent and Trademark Office.

Macmillan Publishing USA
A division of Simon & Schuster, Inc.
1633 Broadway
New York, NY 10019

ISBN 0-7607-0568-2

Text design by Tony Meisel

Printed and bound in the United States of America.

99 00 01 M 9 8 7 6 5 4

RRDC

CONTENTS

INTRODUCTION

SHAKESPEARE'S LIFE

Considering Shakespeare's preeminent place in world litera-
ture, it is astonishing how little we know of his life. What facts
we do have were patched together from official records kept
during Shakespeare's life. We know that William Shakespeare
was baptized on April 26, 1564, as "Gulielmus filius Johannes
Shakspere." The evidence is the parish register of Holy Trinity
Church, Stratford, England.

On November 28, 1582, the Bishop of Worcester issued a
license to William Shakespeare and "Anne Hathwey of
Stratford" to get married, providing that there were no legal
impediments. On May 26, 1583, the records of the parish church
in Stratford note the baptism of Susanna, daughter to William
Shakespeare. On February 2, 1585, the records of the parish
church in Stratford note the baptisms of "Hamnet & Judeth,
sonne and daughter to William Shakspere."

We know that he reached London in the late 1580s and soon
became well known as a playwright and poet. On April 18,
1593, Shakespeare published his long poem *Venus and
Adonis*. It was printed under the author's name and was dedicated to the nineteen-year-old Henry Wriothesley, Earl of
Southampton. On May 9, 1594, another long poem, *The Rape
of Lucrece*, was entered for publication. It also was printed
under Shakespeare's name and was dedicated to the Earl of
Southampton.

In 1594 he helped form a theater company called the Lord
Chamberlain's Men, which in 1603 became the King's Men. In
1603 a garbled and pirated *Hamlet* (now known as Q1) was
printed with Shakespeare's name on the title page. In March
1604, King James gave Shakespeare four yards of red cloth for
a livery, this being in connection with a royal progress through
the City of London. In 1604 a second version of *Hamlet*

appeared, enlarged and corrected, with Shakespeare's name on the title page.

Shakespeare became a partner in the Globe Theatre, where his company performed. He supposedly acted in small parts in his own plays, including the role of the Ghost in *Hamlet*. His success in theater allowed him to purchase a family coat of arms, as well as one of the best houses in Stratford. It was called New Place, and was located in the center of Stratford.

On June 5, 1607, the parish register at Stratford records the marriage of "M. John Hall gentleman & Susanna Shaxspere," the poet's elder daughter. John Hall was a doctor of medicine. On February 21, 1608, the parish register at Holy Trinity, Stratford, records the baptism of Elizabeth Hall, Shakespeare's first grandchild. On September 9, 1608, the parish register at Holy Trinity, Stratford, records the burial of Mary Shakespeare, the poet's mother.

On May 20, 1609, "Shakespeares Sonnets. Never before Imprinted" was entered for publication. On February 10, 1616, the marriage of Judith, Shakespeare's younger daughter, is recorded in the parish register of Holy Trinity, Stratford.

Shakespeare retired to his home town in 1611 and lived there until his death on April 23, 1616. A stone laid over his grave bears the inscription:

> Good Frend for Jesus Sake Forbeare,
> To Digg The Dust Encloased Heare!
> Blest Be The Man That Spares Thes Stones,
> And Curst Be He That Moves My Bones.

These are the records of Shakespeare's life. Shakespeare's biographers may include stories about Shakespeare that have been circulating since at least the seventeenth century, but no one knows whether or not these stories are true. One declares that Shakespeare was an apprentice to a butcher, that he ran away from his master, and was received by actors in London. Another story holds that Shakespeare was a schoolmaster somewhere in the country. Another story has Shakespeare fleeing from his home town to escape the clutches of Sir Thomas Lucy who had often had him whipped and sometimes imprisoned for poaching deer. Yet another story represents the youthful Shakespeare as holding horses and taking care of them while their owners attended the theater. And there are other stories.

WHO WROTE SHAKESPEARE'S PLAYS?

Some people claim that Shakespeare did not write these plays. They argue that someone who had not gone to a university would lack the knowledge to write such beautiful poetry. Some people argue that the seventeenth Earl of Oxford, Edward de Vere, wrote the plays. Others claim it was Sir Francis Bacon. All reputable critics accept that Shakespeare did indeed write the plays attributed to him.

HAMLET: INTRODUCTION

SOURCES OF THE STORY OF HAMLET

The story of Hamlet has been traced back to very early roots in the legends of Iceland, Ireland, and the Scandinavian countries. Tales of Hamlet were gathered and appeared in the thirteenth-century *Historia Danica of Saxo Grammaticus,* which recounts the legendary history of "Amlethus." Printed in 1514, it was freely adapted into French in the fifth volume of François de Belleforest's *Histoires Tragiques,* published in 1576. There was also a play about Hamlet on the English stage by 1589, possibly written by Thomas Kyd. A performance of this older version of *Hamlet,* referred to in modern scholarship as the *Ur-Hamlet,* is recorded for 1594, but the play itself is lost.

EARLY TEXTUAL HISTORY OF SHAKESPEARE'S HAMLET

Basing his story largely upon the account in Belleforest, Shakespeare wrote his version of *Hamlet* in 1601. Its success was so immediate that a pirated version, the so-called "bad quarto," was published in 1603. The corruption and brevity of this text were so great as to necessitate the publication of an authentic copy of the play in 1604. This so-called "good quarto" or "Second Quarto," is almost double the length of the "bad quarto" and is thought to have been printed from Shakespeare's own copy of the play. The third printed version of Shakespeare's play, that in the 1623 folio, is thought to have been printed from the prompt-book of Shakespeare's acting company.

The Second Quarto is generally regarded as the best text but most modern editors collate it with the variants in the First Folio edition for their modern texts of the play. The act, scene and line references used today derive from the work of nineteenth-century editors. Though these divisions are not Shakespeare's own, they are used today to facilitate easy reference.

TRADITION OF REVENGE TRAGEDY

The tradition of revenge tragedy dates back to the Classical Greek drama and in particular to the *Oresteia* of Aeschylus. However, it was through the Latin plays of Seneca that the form became popular, first in the universities and law schools and then in the professional theaters of England. *The Spanish Tragedie* by Thomas Kyd was the first surviving English revenge tragedy. It dates from about 1587. Although this tragedy began with the figure of a Ghost calling for revenge and involved the madness of one of its principal characters, it has otherwise little connection with Shakespeare's *Hamlet*. The next important revenge tragedy was John Marston's *Antonio's Revenge*. Written in 1599, it is the second part of the two-part play entitled *The History of Antonio and Mellida*.

In the character of Antonio, we can see the outlines of Shakespeare's Hamlet. In love with Mellida, Antonio is the son of the King deposed by her usurping father, Piero. Piero is a villain who first seems to agree to their marriage, but then opposes it on the falsified grounds of his daughter's unfaithful lust. Antonio assumes the role of court fool and lets it be known that Antonio has drowned himself for love of Mellida. This breaks her heart and she dies. Depressed over Mellida's death and Piero's pursuit of his mother, Antonio visits his father's tomb, where his cries of suicidal anguish raise up his father's Ghost. The Ghost lays upon him the duty of revenge. When he finally accomplishes his brutal revenge, Marston permits him to continue to live in religious retirement.

Both Antonio and Hamlet have sensitive spirits which are warped by the evils surrounding them. Both of their fathers have lost their thrones; both of their mothers are loved by the rulers who have taken their fathers' places. In addition, both of their own romances are curtailed through the influence of a corrupt court and both are suicidally depressed before and after they have been given the duty of revenge. Finally, both assume the guise of madmen, inflict as great injury as they have received, and are finally vindicated by their authors. The character had already been shaped by Marston when Shakespeare turned his hand to the subject of Hamlet. What Shakespeare did to the character of Revenger was to endow his perception with genius and place him in a context of mystery.

PLOT SUMMARY

Hamlet is the Prince of Denmark. The Ghost of his father tells him that Hamlet's uncle Claudius caused his father's death. A sense of mystery permeates the play's opening with the mysterious appearance of the Ghost. Hamlet is suicidal over the death of his father and the hasty remarriage of his mother to her brother-in-law Claudius, the new King of Denmark.

Brought to meet his father's Ghost, Hamlet pledges to revenge his murder by Claudius who, the Ghost also informs Hamlet, had already committed adultery with his Queen during his lifetime. Though Hamlet accepts the Ghost's word while he is with him, seeds of doubt about the Ghost's authenticity have been sown from the very beginning of the play and continue to torment Hamlet for much of its remainder. Hamlet wonders if the Ghost is actually a diabolic impersonation of the spirit of Hamlet's father come to tempt him to his damnation.

The better to investigate Claudius' guilt, Hamlet assumes the guise of madness, though the sight of his father's spirit has caused his already unstable spirit to totter on the brink of actual insanity. This combination of real and assumed mental instability so worries Claudius that he begins to spy on Hamlet to see if Hamlet represents a danger to him. He first sets Rosencrantz and Guildenstern to spy on Hamlet and then spies upon a prearranged meeting between Hamlet and his estranged sweetheart, Ophelia.

Meanwhile, Hamlet has thought of a new means to test

Claudius' guilt and the authenticity of the Ghost; he will stage a performance of a play which will reproduce Claudius' crime and observe his reaction to it. This plan is successful as Claudius breaks down during the performance, but since the performance also alerts Claudius to Hamlet's knowledge of his crime and consequent danger to him, he exiles Hamlet to England. Claudius' chief adviser, Polonius, convinces Claudius to let him spy on Hamlet before he is exiled. Hamlet's mother, Gertrude, calls Hamlet to her room, where Polonius will be hidden to overhear the conference.

For the two months since Hamlet has seen the Ghost, Hamlet has been unable to commit his vowed revenge. Unable to explain to himself either his long delay or his depression, he has investigated this problem as eagerly as Claudius and Polonius. He had first rationalized his delay on the grounds of doubt about the Ghost's nature. But after Claudius breaks down during the play, Hamlet is sure of his stepfather's guilt. Hamlet has a perfect opportunity to achieve his revenge when he accidentally comes upon the guilt-ridden Claudius alone in prayer. Again he rationalizes himself into delay, this time on the grounds that his revenge would not be horrible enough as Claudius' penitence might save his soul from hell.

Hamlet then goes to his mother's room, but he is in such an unnaturally excited state that he scares his mother and the hidden Polonius into crying for help. In anger he madly lashes out at the hidden figure, resulting in Polonius' death. This unpremeditated act seals Hamlet's own doom.

Claudius alters his order for Hamlet's exile so that Hamlet will be executed in England. While on shipboard to England, however, Hamlet again acts rashly; he discovers the letter ordering his death and changes it so that the bearers, Rosencrantz and Guildenstern, will be put to death in his place. His success in this wild enterprise leads him to the religious perception that "There's a divinity that shapes our ends,/Rough-hew them how we will."

Escaping from the ship during an attack upon it by pirates, he returns to Denmark with a clear conscience both about his coming revenge against Claudius and his own order for the executions of Rosencrantz and Guildenstern. But he makes no plans for his revenge since he has come to place his full confidence upon Providence. This is not true, however, of Claudius or of Laertes, Polonius' son, who has also returned to Denmark to revenge his own father's death. Forewarned by Hamlet of his return, they lay plans for his death through a fencing match in which Laertes will use an illegally sharp and poisoned sword backed up by a poisoned drink. Laertes' grievance against Hamlet is increased by the madness and death of his sister, Ophelia, and by Hamlet's aggressive behavior toward him when they meet at her funeral.

Claudius' and Laertes' plans backfire. As a result, Hamlet, Gertrude, Claudius, and Laertes are all killed. At the cost of his own life, Hamlet has, however, achieved his revenge in terms that exonerate his soul from the danger of damnation into which Claudius seems to be sunk. Celebrated for his nobility of spirit, Hamlet is given a hero's funeral.

HAMLET
ACT I

ACT I: SCENE 1

The play opens at a sentry post before the castle of Elsinore, Denmark, during medieval times. It is midnight and Francisco, a sentry, is at his post awaiting the changing of the guard. Bernardo enters and asks, "Who's there?" Francisco challenges him for the password, saying, "Nay, answer me; stand, and unfold yourself."

COMMENT

These opening two lines are significant because they set a tone of watchful suspicion. This is later to characterize the major characters and their supporters: Hamlet, with the aid of Horatio, spies on Claudius, while Claudius, with the aid of Rosencrantz, Guildenstern, Polonius, Ophelia and Gertrude, spies on Hamlet. On a minor level, Polonius also spies on his son, Laertes.

Horatio and Marcellus, who will share Bernardo's sentry duty this evening, now enter. Horatio is not a regular sentry but has been asked by Marcellus to join the watch with them because of something unusual which has occurred on the two previous nights for which they wish his opinion and help. Marcellus tells Bernardo that Horatio has rejected their story as "fantasy" and will not allow himself to believe it.

COMMENT

These few remarks help to define Horatio's character. We later learn that Horatio is a Stoic, a follower of an ancient Greek and Roman philosophy that held that the pain of life could be overcome by the suppression of all personal desire, by remaining unmoved by joy or grief, and by submitting without complaint to what was unavoidable. Horatio's skeptical turn of mind is also suggested here. This reveals itself in his refusal to accept superstitious hearsay evidence.

Marcellus explains the "dreaded sight" that has appeared before them the last two nights. Before he and Bernardo have half begun their tale, the Ghost enters. Horatio agrees with the two sentries that the Ghost, who is dressed in armor, looks like the dead King Hamlet. Marcellus suggests that since Horatio is a "scholar," he should be the one to know how to speak to the Ghost. Horatio does this, beginning by asking the Ghost, "What art thou?" and closing with the challenge, "by heaven I charge thee, speak!" But Marcellus notes that "It is offended," and Bernardo that "it stalks away." Now that his own eyes have seen the Ghost, Horatio admits that it is "something more than fantasy" and that it forebodes "some strange eruption to our state," some coming disaster.

Marcellus asks Horatio whether he knows why there is such a strict watch and why the country is so busy building armaments. Horatio replies that the late King Fortinbras of Norway, jealous of the martial conquests of the late Danish King Hamlet, challenged the Danish King to combat, staking all his possessions on the outcome, and that the late Hamlet killed Fortinbras and took over his forfeited lands as had been agreed. Recently, however, young Fortinbras, son of the slain King, had raised an unlawful army to recover by force of arms the territories his father had lost to the Danes. It is against such a possibility, Horatio thinks, that the present Danish military preparations have been undertaken. Bernardo agrees with this and further suggests that it may be in connection with these wars, with which the late King Hamlet is still so involved, that his Ghost has now been aroused. Horatio is not so sure of this as he is troubled by the memory of similar supernatural occurrences before the murder of Julius Caesar: Ghosts in the Roman streets, comets, bloody dews, ominous signs in the sun, and a lengthy eclipse of the moon. He suggests that "heaven and earth" are demonstrating a similar "omen" to "feared events" for their own country.

COMMENT

Shakespeare had placed much importance on these supernatural occurrences in two of his other tragedies, *Julius Caesar* and *Macbeth*. This suggests that Shakespeare is using these supernatural appearances not only to thrill and amaze the "groundlings" (the poor, uneducated part of the audience that stood on the ground before the stage to watch the performance), but also to suggest that the whole universe is disrupted by human evil and will work in mysterious ways to right the balance of nature.

At this point the Ghost reenters and Horatio, recognizing the danger involved, vows to cross it even if it destroys him. He challenges the Ghost to speak to him, but only on certain conditions. He first proposes, "If there be any good thing to be done/That may to thee do ease and grace to me,/Speak to me." The second condition under which Horatio will permit the Ghost to speak to him is if he has some secret knowledge of his country's fate which his country might avoid by being told of it. Third, he will let the Ghost speak if the Ghost wishes to reveal the hiding place of any treasure he may have buried. Before the Ghost can answer, however, the cock crows and, as the three characters try vainly with their swords to force the Ghost to stand and answer the questions, the Ghost fades away. Horatio notes that he has often heard that at the cock's warning of the approach of day the "erring spirit" must return "to his confine." The Ghost's disappearance seems to confirm the truth of this saying. Marcellus agrees, but further notes that there are those who say that at the Christmas season . . .

Wherein our Saviour's birth is celebrated,
This bird of dawning singeth all night long,
And then, they say, no spirit dare stir abroad,
The nights are wholesome, then no planets strike,
No fairy takes, nor witch hath power to charm.
So hallowed and so gracious is that time.

COMMENT

The last speech suggests that there is tension between Christianity and supernatural manifestations such as Ghosts. Furthermore, we have seen that Horatio was very careful in confronting the Ghost to guard himself against any evil power it might possess. In his first confrontation, he charged the Ghost to disclose his true nature and to speak to him "by heaven." In his second confrontation, he charges the Ghost only to speak to him if he wishes him to do a good thing which will bring him grace. Horatio's behavior suggests the Ghost's morally questionable nature and serves as a Christian model against which Hamlet's later confrontation with the Ghost may be judged.

Since it is now morning, Horatio suggests they go tell Hamlet what they have seen, for he suspects that "This spirit, dumb to us, will speak to him." Marcellus agrees and they depart from the stage.

SUMMARY

This opening scene has the following important purposes:

1. It serves as an "exposition" to set forth the important occurrences which precede the beginning of the play: the war between Norway and Denmark which the late King Hamlet won, young Fortinbras' military preparations to regain Norway's lost territories, and Denmark's counter-military preparations.

2. It provides an exciting and suspenseful beginning by introducing the ominous and silent Ghost who will motivate the action of the entire play.

3. It raises some questions as to the nature and importance of supernatural manifestations in general and of this Ghost in particular. It also questions the relation of such manifestations to Christianity, questions which will be raised repeatedly throughout the play.

4. It introduces us to Horatio, a skeptical Stoic, who is Hamlet's closest friend. Horatio serves as a contrast to Hamlet.

ACT I: SCENE 2

The second scene opens the next day. King Claudius and the important members of his court enter a room of state in the castle at Elsinore. Claudius begins the scene with a formal public address to his court which touches on the important matters of state before him.

First, Claudius takes up his hasty marriage to his brother's widow, Queen Gertrude. He explains that, as she has an equal right to the throne and as his own desires also favored her, he has married her even though it is less than two months since the death of her husband and his brother, the late King Hamlet. He admits that it might have been more fitting for him and the whole kingdom to remain in mourning for the late King rather than to celebrate a marriage, but he states that he has only proceeded in this matter because his chief counselors of state had freely advised him to do so, for which he thanks them.

The second item of state, and the real reason for this meeting, concerns the activities of young Fortinbras, of which we have already learned something in the first scene. We are now told that Fortinbras, believing Denmark to be disorganized and weak as a result of the death of King Hamlet, had sent several messages to Claudius demanding the surrender of the lands lost by his father. Claudius responded by sending an envoy to the King of Norway, the uncle of young Fortinbras, who, old and bedridden, has scarcely heard of the unlawful activities of his nephew. In the letter, Claudius demands that he suppress his nephew's unlawful activities, further suggesting that the cost of rearming Norway is coming out of the King of Norway's own revenues and that he had better look into this matter. Claudius now dispatches Cornelius and Voltemand to carry this letter to the King of Norway as quickly as possible. The third item is the personal request of Laertes, son of the Lord Chamberlain, Polonius, to be permitted to return to Paris, from which he had come to attend Claudius' coronation.

Before Claudius allows Laertes to make his request, he tells him how willing he is to grant him any request because of the great respect the throne of Denmark holds for his father. Upon learning the nature of the request, Claudius refers the decision to Polonius, who gives his consent to his son's leaving, which is then seconded by Claudius.

COMMENT

Claudius' opening speech is majestic, balanced, and controlled, indicating similar qualities in his character. These qualities may help to explain why he was elected to the throne of Denmark over the claim of his nephew, Hamlet, son to the late King Hamlet (for the King of Denmark was elected to the throne by the nobility from among the members of the royal family). His imposing statesmanship is further indicated by his activities since gaining the throne, as shown in this speech. He has only fulfilled his personal desire to marry Gertrude after gaining the cooperation and support of his chief counselors, one of whom, Polonius, we here see him treating with exaggerated marks of deference.

Claudius, then, appears to be an able politician as regards members of his own court. But, more than this, he is also a statesman. Although he is preparing for war, he prefers to avoid war if it is possible to do so through diplomatic means. As we shall later learn, his letter to the King of Norway is successful in accomplishing this purpose. Fortinbras' conjectures as to the weak and disorganized state of Denmark appear completely false as Claudius, in less than two months of rule, has ably taken the situation in hand.

Claudius now turns to the last item of business, the desire of his nephew, now stepson, Hamlet, to return to his studies in Wittenberg. But as Claudius addresses him with the words "my cousin Hamlet, and my son," Hamlet says to himself, "A little more than kin, and less than kind!"

COMMENT

In Hamlet's first silent speech (called an "aside" in the stage directions), we learn something of the quality of his mind. Here, Hamlet is making a bitter little joke to himself. This joke is based upon a pun on the meanings of the word "kind." In the seventeenth century, when Hamlet was written, the word "kind" meant that which pertains to "kindred," especially those feelings of care and concern which blood relations should feel for each other. When Hamlet uses the word "kind," then, he is referring to both "kindness" in our sense of the term and "kinship." Claudius, then is "a little more than kin," since he is now also Hamlet's stepfather. He is also a little less than kin, in the older sense of the term "kind," the "kindness" associated with blood relations. This bitter joke conveys Hamlet's suspicions regarding Claudius' integrity: first, that though Claudius may be acting with a show of kindred concern, his feelings for him are far from fatherly, and second, that his feelings for Hamlet's true father may have been far from brotherly, though how far Hamlet does not dare suggest even to himself.

Claudius now asks Hamlet how it is that he is still in mourning. Hamlet quickly retorts that his mourning is not sufficient. His mother begs him to put off his mourning attire and gloom and look with more friendliness upon Claudius, to seek in him rather than in the dust for his father, and, finally, to accept his natural father's death. Gertrude next asks why his father's death seems so special to him, not understanding that the very commonness of death may increase rather than diminish Hamlet's despair. Hamlet picks up her innocent use of the word "seems" to disclaim any such false appearance: "Seems, madam? Nay, it is. I know not 'seems.' "

His full mourning is not simply an outward show, since his inner feelings go beyond all such external appearances:

"I have that within which passeth show," he says. Claudius says that it is good for a son to give such mourning duties to his father as long as they are held to some prescribed term but that to continue beyond such a time is impious and unmanly. Claudius says, "It shows a will most incorrect to heaven" since it stubbornly refuses to accept the will of heaven. Claudius begs Hamlet to put aside his mourning, to think of him as his father for he does feel toward Hamlet as a father, and to make him happy by remaining beside him in Denmark rather than returning to Wittenberg. The Queen seconds this desire on her own account and Hamlet replies that he will obey her. Claudius is so delighted with this unforced reply that he vows to spend the evening toasting Hamlet's apparent reconciliation with him. With this, the formal audience is over and the King and court depart from the stage, leaving Hamlet alone.

We have now arrived at Hamlet's first "soliloquy," a term for the Elizabethan stage convention which permits a character to tell the audience his inner thoughts. Hamlet begins with the anguished wish that his "solid" (some scholars, following Kittredge, would substitute "sullied" here as the word Shakespeare originally intended) "flesh would melt" away by itself. Since this cannot be, he wishes that God had not given a direct law forbidding suicide. He continues with an anguished general cry against the will of heaven: "O God, God,/How weary, stale, flat, and unprofitable/Seem to me all the uses of this world!" He is led to this cry of despair by his recent recognition that justice does not rule the world, that "things rank and gross in nature/possess it merely."

The world appears to him in this light because his "excellent" father has died and Claudius, so far inferior to his father, has succeeded to his place, not only to his father's throne but also to his wife. But it is his mother's behavior which has most disillusioned him. His father had been "so loving" and gentle to his mother. She had seemed to return his affection and "would hang on him" as if the more she was with him the more her "appetite" for him would grow. (Note that Hamlet expresses his father's feelings for his mother as "love" but his mother's feelings for his father as "appetite," a sign of his new awareness of the "grossness" of nature in general and of his mother in particular.) Not only that, she had seemed genuinely overcome by grief at his father's funeral. "And yet within a month" she had married. The thought is so horrifying to him that he tries to close it out from his mind, "Let me not think on't," for as soon as he does think of it he must condemn his mother and, with her, all women: "frailty, thy name is woman."

The fact that his parents' happy marriage now seems to have been a delusion shows Hamlet that he did not know the true nature of the person closest to him, his mother. If he cannot even trust his own mother, there is no one he may trust. In the past two months, then, he has realized two terrible facts of human existence through his loved ones: the fact of death and the fact of human imperfection and falseness. These have so disillusioned him with the value of life that he has sunk completely into a suicidal state of mind. He is particularly heartbroken over his mother's behavior and he can do nothing about it: "It is not, nor it cannot come to good./But break my heart, for I must hold my tongue."

At this point Horatio enters with Marcellus and Bernardo. Hamlet quickly rouses himself from his suicidal reflections and is delighted to see Horatio, a fellow student of his at the University of Wittenberg whom he holds in high regard. Asked what he is doing in Elsinore, Horatio replies that "I came to see your father's funeral." Hamlet ironically returns: "Do not mock me fellow student./I think it was to see my mother's wedding." When Horatio agrees that it followed quickly upon the funeral, Hamlet replies with further satiric bite: "Thrift, thrift, Horatio/The funeral baked meats/Did coldly furnish forth the marriage tables." Then he more seriously expresses his displeasure.

COMMENT

In the past scene we have seen rapid shifts in Hamlet's

moods. First he reflects satirically to himself on the nature of Claudius; then he expresses himself in a melancholy fashion to his mother on the subject of his continuing mourning. Thirdly, he reflects in a melancholy fashion to himself on his desire for suicide as a result of his mother's remarriage. Lastly, he expresses himself satirically to Horatio on the subject of his mother's remarriage. We see, first, that he is both satiric and melancholy to himself and to others, depending upon his particular mood at the moment. Secondly, we see that he alternates between these two moods that have a special relationship to one another.

Whether directed with murderous or suicidal intent, this destructive impulse shows, in Claudius' words, "a will most incorrect to heaven," for both of these desires are equally forbidden by religious law. As Hamlet states in his first soliloquy, his religious beliefs forbid him to commit suicide. Since death is so common that it expresses the will of heaven, Claudius asks Hamlet: "Why should we in our peevish opposition/Take it to heart?" But this is exactly Hamlet's condition; the evil in the universe has suddenly come home to him and he does "take it to heart." He cannot accept the will of heaven in this regard and yet, as he will not actively oppose God, his opposition is reduced to frustrated peevishness which expresses itself in alternating moods and satire and melancholy.

Horatio now tells Hamlet that a Ghost looking like his father has appeared three times before the midnight sentries at their guard post and that he had been present at the last visitation. Hamlet questions Horatio minutely about the Ghost's appearance. Convinced of its similarity to his father, Hamlet resolves to appear at the watch that night. He vows: "If it assume my noble father's person,/I'll speak to it though hell itself should gape."

COMMENT

At the time when *Hamlet* was written, rather than in the legendary time in which it was set, the University of Wittenberg was a center of Protestant theology. With historical inconsistency, Shakespeare casts his legendary character, Hamlet, as a student at a contemporary university. As a student at Wittenberg, Hamlet would have been taught the orthodox Protestant position on Ghosts: they were not the spirits of the deceased but either angels or devils who took on the appearance of a deceased person to tempt a surviving relative into spiritual damnation. Whereas Horatio had originally accepted the more extreme, skeptical position that Ghosts do not exist, Hamlet approaches his coming meeting with the Ghost with the belief that it is probably a devil who has taken on his father's form in order to damn him to hell. He is willing to risk this danger to learn the Ghost's message.

Hamlet asks the guards to tell no one of the appearance of the Ghost, saying that he will reward them for their silence. He sets up a meeting for that night and bids them farewell. They leave. Alone on the stage, Hamlet expresses his suspicion that there has been "some foul play," a reechoing of his earlier, half-thought suspicion.

SUMMARY

This scene accomplishes the following purposes:
1. It introduces the play's two leading characters, Claudius and Hamlet, whom Hamlet is later to call "mighty opposites." Claudius seems immensely capable of dealing with the problems of state and of life. He has established an ordered, efficient state and diplomatically avoids war. He preaches to Hamlet the acceptance of life with all its evils. Hamlet is shown to be a brilliant, sensitive, highly erratic, and moody person who refuses to accept life's imperfections and has been driven into a suicidal frame of mind by his father's death and his mother's infidelity.

2. By the end of the scene, Hamlet, despite his personal withdrawal, has become involved in the action. He has complied with Claudius' request to remain at the Danish court rather than return to Wittenberg as he had desired, and he has resolved to speak with the Ghost and learn its bidding even though it damn him (further indication of the uncertain nature of the Ghost).

ACT I: SCENE 3

The scene is set in Polonius' rooms within the castle at Elsinore later that day. Laertes is about to leave for Paris and is bidding his sister, Ophelia, farewell. In a long speech, he warns her not to trust Hamlet's intentions toward her and to protect her chastity. Even though Hamlet may say he loves her and perhaps now does, he cannot marry as he wishes since he is of royal birth and is thus far above her. She answers that she will follow his advice but that he should not simply preach strictness to her and then act like a libertine himself.

At this point Polonius enters, surprised that Laertes is still there since the wind is up and the boat is waiting for him. He hurries him to go, gives him his blessing, and then delays his departure with moral commonplaces: he should be discreet in words and action, devote himself to true friends rather than every new acquaintance, and avoid quarrels but, once involved, bear himself strongly. Polonius also tells his son to listen to all but reserve his true thoughts only to a few, accept other men's criticism but refrain from criticizing others, and dress with an elegance that is not gaudy, for appearance is often used as a guide to the nature of a man. He concludes that "This above all, to thine own self be true,/And it must follow as the night the day/Thou canst not then be false to any man."

COMMENT

We see that Laertes takes after his father in long-winded, moral preaching. Polonius appears foolish in this regard. He comes out, hurrying Laertes to leave, "Yet here, Laertes? Aboard, aboard, for shame!" But then he delays him with standard moralizing. This speech does not reflect the wise fruits of a lifetime of reflection. Even though Polonius claims integrity to be the most important moral quality, he is himself the falsest of men, as we shall later see.

Laertes finally leaves, bidding Ophelia to "remember well/ What I have said to you." Polonius questions Ophelia as to what this is and she tells him that it concerns Hamlet. This reminds Polonius that he has been told of the meetings between Hamlet and Ophelia and asks her what is between them. To her reply that Hamlet has recently given her many signs of his "affection," Polonius expresses disgust: "Affection? Pooh!" He tells her that she is just an innocent girl if she believes Hamlet's intentions.

When she says that he has spoken to her of "love/In honorable fashion," Polonius says that this is just a trap to seduce her. To protect his daughter's honor and his own, he tells her first that she should not see Hamlet so often; rather, she should play harder to get. As he continues to explain the ways of men to his innocent daughter, he becomes more and more convinced of her danger until he suddenly decides that she must not see him again and so commands her. She is an obedient daughter and agrees to obey him, at which time they leave the stage.

COMMENT

Polonius' lack of true wisdom, suggested earlier, is here confirmed. He does not investigate the nature of Hamlet's intentions but assumes that they must be dishonorable and that a marriage between the Prince and his daughter would be impossible. We later learn that he was wrong on both counts: at Ophelia's funeral, Gertrude says that she had hoped Ophelia would be Hamlet's

wife and Hamlet proclaims his love for her. Furthermore, Polonius' sudden decision not to permit his daughter to see Hamlet again, a decision arrived at without
any considered judgment, is a serious error, as he later
admits, since it serves to reinforce Hamlet's disillusionment with women. This, in turn, helps to break Ophelia's
heart and destroy her sanity. In his relations with his
daughter, Polonius shows an overbearing authority and
apparent worldly wisdom without true discretion.

SUMMARY

This scene serves the following purposes:
1. It introduces us more fully to the important character of
Polonius and shows him to be a foolish, authoritarian old
man. His foolish self-importance, which is even more fully
revealed later on, causes him to be treated in many instances
as a comic character. But his effects and end are far from
comic.
2. It also introduces us to Ophelia, an innocent, obedient young
girl, and to the fact of Hamlet's love for her.
3. The action of the scene is important in so far as Polonius'
decision to restrict his daughter from seeing Hamlet bars
Hamlet's love from any normal development it might have
had. This also seriously hurts Ophelia.

ACT I: SCENES 4 AND 5

Hamlet, Horatio, and Marcellus enter the platform before the
castle where the sentry post is situated. It is midnight and
some trumpets are sounding. Horatio asks Hamlet what it
means and Hamlet replies that the King and court are spend-
ing the evening drinking and that every time Claudius makes
a toast, the trumpets and drums sound. Horatio asks whether
this is a Danish custom and Hamlet says that it is, but
although he is a native here "and to the manner born," he
thinks it better not to keep this time-honored custom which
has given Denmark a reputation for drunkenness among other
nations.

COMMENT

In Scene 2, Claudius had referred to his habitual evening drinking when he said that once "again" he would make loud toasts with wine that evening in honor of his reconciliation with Hamlet. When Hamlet greeted Horatio he said to him: "We'll teach you to drink deep ere you depart." Here we see another difference between Claudius and Hamlet; Claudius indulges in sensual pleasure while Hamlet views such indulgence with puritanical disgust.

Hamlet explains that, just as Denmark's positive achievements are overshadowed by its reputation for drunkenness, so it can happen in the case of particular men. A personality defect with which a person is born, and for which they cannot be held guilty, may so develop that it leads to irrational behavior. Or, a bad habit may similarly overcome the control of their reason. Then such men, carrying "the stamp of one defect," though they have all other virtues, will come under general condemnation for this one fault.

COMMENT

This has generally been taken to represent Shakespeare's discussion of the "tragic flaw." This concept holds that the proper tragic hero is one who is above average in virtue but is brought to tragedy as a result of one flaw in his character. Critics are in greater agreement about the meaning of this passage than about the nature of Hamlet's supposed "tragic flaw."

At this point the Ghost enters. Hamlet calls upon the angels to defend him and then addresses the Ghost. Hamlet says that whether the Ghost is an angel come from heaven with charitable intent, or a damned spirit come from hell with wicked intent, the question is so uncertain that he will speak to him as though he were the true spirit of his father. Hamlet asks the Ghost why he has returned from death. The Ghost, rather than answer him, silently beckons Hamlet to follow. Horatio and Marcellus advise Hamlet not to follow the Ghost, but Hamlet says he has nothing to fear since "I do not set my life at a pin's fee." Horatio says that the Ghost might tempt him to the edge of the cliff, drive him mad, and then cause him to commit suicide (possibilities which might follow if the Ghost were a devil). But Hamlet answers, "My fate cries out," and, breaking away from Horatio and Marcellus, who are now physically holding him back, he follows the Ghost to another part of the platform, leaving the stage.

Though Marcellus now says, "Something is rotten in the state of Denmark," Horatio hopes the coming of the Ghost may have a blessed effect. He says, "Heaven will direct it." In any case, they decide it is not fit to leave Hamlet alone and they follow him.

The fifth scene begins with the entrance of the Ghost on another part of the platform. Hamlet follows but then tells the Ghost to stop and speak because he will follow him no further. The Ghost turns and now finally reveals that he is the true spirit of Hamlet's father, doomed for a certain term to purgatory. He has returned to earth to tell Hamlet that if he ever loved his father he should "Revenge his foul and most unnatural murder."

COMMENT

Up to this point we have noted three different attitudes toward Ghosts: Marcellus' superstitious belief in the existence of Ghosts without too much certainty as to their nature; Horatio's initial disbelief in the existence of Ghosts; and Hamlet's Protestant belief that Ghosts are the appearance of angels or devils in the assumed form of a deceased person. Now we see the fourth possible Renaissance attitude toward Ghosts, the Catholic position that Ghosts are the true spirits of deceased persons who are in purgatory. This is the position the Ghost holds of himself, though this does not necessarily mean that he is telling Hamlet the truth. Whatever be the truth of the matter (and the doubt is to continue to torment Hamlet), the Ghost is acting in a traditional way by calling for revenge.

Upon learning of his father's murder, Hamlet is anxious to learn the name of his murderer that he may be "swift" in his revenge. But when the Ghost reveals that the murderer is Claudius, Hamlet exclaims, "O my prophetic soul!" This indicates that Hamlet had dimly suspected as much, as was earlier shown. The Ghost now reveals that Claudius had seduced his "most seeming-virtuous queen" to "shameful lust" before his death. And the Ghost agrees with Hamlet as to the relative merits of Claudius and himself when he says: "O Hamlet, what a falling-off was there." Though he considers Claudius "a wretch whose natural gifts were poor/To those of mine," he also understands that lust will leave "a radiant angel" to "prey on garbage."

He then explains how he was killed. He says he was sleeping in his orchard in the afternoon when Claudius poured poison in his ear. This quickly killed him. "Most horrible" of all, Claudius' murder deprived him of the opportunity to confess and take the Sacraments before death. He now tells Hamlet that if he has any natural feeling for his father he should not allow his murderer to live and, what is even worse, turn his royal bed into a couch for incestuous lust. Whatever Hamlet does, however, he should not "taint" his mind by even contemplating anything against his mother but "leave her to heaven" and to her own conscience. As morning is coming, he bids Hamlet a quick farewell with the words, "Remember me."

COMMENT

Apart from the actual story of the murder and adultery, the Ghost did not tell Hamlet anything he did not already suspect. What's more, the telling was done exactly in terms of Hamlet's own values, as shown in his first soliloquy. There, his father's attributes were held to be far superior to those of Claudius, his mother's lustful change was viewed with disgust, and greater emphasis was placed upon the horror of his mother's infidelity than upon his father's death. This suggests one of two possibilities: either Hamlet takes after his father, as Laertes does after his, or that the Ghost is simply telling Hamlet what he wants to hear, justifying his most horrible imaginings so that he may have a reason to take direct action which may damn him. Even the true piece of information he gives him, the manner of the murder, is something that a devil would know and might use to tempt Hamlet to his damnation.

Hamlet's immediate response is to call for help upon all the host of heaven and the earth, and then he has the terrible suspicion that perhaps he had better also call upon the help of hell in remembering his father. But he rejects this suspicion that the Ghost may come from hell; "And shall I couple hell? O fie!" Taking hold of himself, he vows to wipe everything from his memory except his father's commandment to revenge his murder. But as he thinks of his evil mother and still more of Claudius, a "villain, villain, smiling, damnèd villain," he begins to lose control of his reason.

He feels he has discovered a wonderful truth that he must write down in the notebook he carries with him to record memorable sayings, and he writes, "that one may smile, and smile, and be a villain." Such a statement is, of course, neither a brilliant discovery nor an especially well-phrased observation and so would not normally be written down. But that Hamlet is not in a normal frame of mind is immediately shown when he responds to his friends' calling to him with a falconer's cry used for summoning his hawk: "Hillo, ho, ho, boy! Come, bird, come." They ask him for his news and, after pledging them to secrecy, reveals that any "villain dwelling in all

Denmark" is a thorough "knave" or scoundrel. To this Horatio well responds: "There needs no Ghost, my lord, come from the grave/To tell us this." Hamlet agrees and somewhat hysterically says that they should part, the others to their business and he to pray. Horatio notes: "These are but wild and whirling words, my lord," again indicating that Hamlet is not in a rational state.

Hamlet collects himself for a moment and tells them that "it is an honest Ghost," that is, the true spirit of his father rather than a devil who has assumed his form, but that he cannot tell them what he and the Ghost said to each other. He now asks them once again to swear that they will never reveal what they have seen tonight, but they feel insulted that Hamlet should ask them again what they have already promised him. Hamlet now wants them to formally swear to this upon his sword and, as they hesitate, the Ghost cries from under the stage, "Swear." This once again unsettles Hamlet's reason and he becomes hysterical, saying to the Ghost: "Ha, ha, boy, say'st thou so? Art thou there, truepenny?" He tells them to swear as they "hear this fellow in the cellarage." They shift ground but the Ghost continues to follow them under the stage, repeatedly telling them to "swear by his sword." At this point Hamlet exclaims to the Ghost: "Well said, old mole! Canst work i' th' earth so fast?/A worthy pioner!"

COMMENT

During his meeting with the Ghost, Hamlet was convinced that this was the true spirit of his father. Immediately thereafter, as he is swearing by heaven that he will carry out his father's command, a slight suspicion rises that it may after all have been a devil from hell. He rejects this idea, but as he thinks of his revenge, his mind becomes unsettled, a possibility Horatio had stressed in the event the Ghost proved to be an evil spirit. Hamlet gains control of his reason and tells Horatio that the Ghost was "honest" rather than a devil, but as the Ghost cries out from several places beneath the platform, Hamlet's reason again becomes unsettled and he treats the Ghost as though he were a familiar devil with whom he had made a pact.

Devils were often compared to "moles" in that they worked underground and were even thought to mine for treasure. Furthermore, Hamlet's complete lack of respect would not be fitting to the true Ghost of his father. However much Hamlet's reason may tell him that this is "an honest Ghost," then, he has a lurking suspicion that it may, in fact, be a devil and this suspicion acts to unsettle his reason. In addition, the Ghost not only acts like a devil in the last part of the scene, but his effect upon Hamlet has been devilish. This continues the audience's own uncertainty as to the Ghost's true nature.

Hamlet once more returns to rationality, but his unsettling experience with the supernatural causes him to tell Horatio: "There are more things in heaven and earth, Horatio,/Than are dreamt of in your philosophy." Though the supernatural appears mysterious to Hamlet, his experience with it causes him to grant it a validity which Horatio's earlier skepticism would have denied. Hamlet now tells them that they should be careful not to give any indication by look or word that they know anything about this night because Hamlet may later think it necessary "to put an antic disposition on," that is, to act as though he were insane.

COMMENT

As Hamlet does periodically act insanely for much of the remainder of the play and here says that he is going to consciously pretend madness for his own purposes, the question has long been argued as to the true nature of Hamlet's madness. Though this question can never be answered with any certainty, the fact that Hamlet's sanity had begun to totter before he got the idea of playing mad is significant. It suggests that Hamlet may have decided to play mad because he is afraid of actually going mad and can use the role of madness to mask and relieve his true psychological instability. It is true that in the original story the Hamlet character assumes the role of madness to further his secret investigation of the King, but Shakespeare's Hamlet makes little if any use of his assumed madness in this way, and so the psychological interpretation of Hamlet's assumed madness seems more justified.

Horatio and Marcellus now formally swear to keep Hamlet's two secrets, the meeting with the Ghost and Hamlet's assumed madness, and they now prepare to part. Before leaving, however, Hamlet says, "The time is out of joint. O cursèd spite/ That ever I was born to set it right!"

COMMENT

Hamlet sees his mission of revenge as one of social reform. We have seen this impulse to change the world rather than to accept its evils in his earlier moments of satire, and the Ghost has now given this impulse a positive direction and purpose. However much part of Hamlet may desire to cause a drastic change in the world, the other part of him desires only to withdraw from this evil world and may provide a constitutional hindrance to the easy accomplishment of his assigned task. When the Ghost first appeared, Hamlet had said: "My fate cries out." But now he considers it spiteful of fate to have assigned him a task so difficult for a person like himself to carry out—how difficult we shall see in the remainder of the play.

SUMMARY

These two scenes accomplish the following purposes in closing the first act:
1. Claudius, who impressed us favorably in the second scene, is now revealed to have murdered his brother after having

committed adultery with his wife. This places his Christian advice to Hamlet about accepting the evil of the world as the will of heaven in a new light.

2. Hamlet is given the task to revenge his father's murder and rid his court of evil. This task is given supernatural sanction, which may indicate that, as Horatio said, "Heaven will direct it." This is especially possible since Claudius has been shown to be an improper spokesman for the will of heaven. There are, however, strong counter suggestions that the Ghost may be a devil and that Hamlet may be endangering his life and soul in following his commands.

3. Two reasons are given which may help to explain Hamlet's later delay in carrying out his assigned task:

a. These scenes establish the Ghost's uncertain nature. Hamlet's own uncertainty has already troubled him to the point of mental instability.

b. They also show Hamlet's melancholic and generally unstable state of mind. The former quality causes Hamlet to feel that he is personally unsuited to the active role of the revenger; the latter, already increased to near insanity by his confusing encounter with the Ghost, may make it difficult for him to concentrate rationally upon the act of revenge.

4. The act had begun by showing us first an ominous Ghost and then an apparently well-ordered state. It ends with Hamlet in the Ghost's power, sworn to overthrow the state, mentally unstable, and considering further assuming the role of madness. The action of the play, the course of Hamlet's revenge, has now been determined. The introduction of situation, characters, and theme now completed, the stage is set for action.

HAMLET
ACT II

ACT II: SCENE 1

We are once again in Polonius' rooms. Polonius is sending off his servant, Reynaldo, to Paris with money and letters for his son, Laertes. He tells Reynaldo that he should inquire about Laertes' behavior before he visits him. Reynaldo, who seems to know his master's ways very well, tells Polonius that he had already intended to do this and is well praised for this in turn. Polonius now instructs Reynaldo in some of the refinements of spying.

Reynaldo is to find some of Laertes' Danish acquaintances and casually bring up the subject of Laertes. He is then to suggest that Laertes is a libertine, that he gambles, duels, swears, and goes to brothels. Reynaldo objects that this would dishonor Laertes, but Polonius explains that this will draw out, either by agreement or denial, the truth about Laertes' behavior as the others have seen it. In the middle of this explanation, Polonius forgets what he wants to say and Reynaldo has to remind him of what he had just said. Polonius then concludes, with a generalization about his tactics, that it is wisdom to be devious in approaching one's target for one can best "by indirections find directions out." Satisfied that Reynaldo has learned his lesson, Polonius bids him good-bye but with a final order to make sure that Laertes is keeping up his musical studies.

COMMENT

In this scene we see the absent-minded old man give Reynaldo the true fruits of his life-long experience, not the high moralizing about integrity he gave to Laertes, but the knowledge of successful spying and falsehood which has become almost second nature to him. His conclusion is doubly significant to the play, for we shall see that all attempts at direct planning are doomed to failure.

Ophelia now enters. She is very frightened because as she was sewing alone in her room, Hamlet had entered in a very disordered state, his jacket unlaced, without a hat, his stockings dirty and hanging down ungartered to his ankles, his knees knocking together, "And with a look so piteous in purport/As if he had been loosèd out of hell/To speak of horrors." He had taken hold of her wrist and held her hard at arm's length with one hand while his other hand was held over his brow. Staying a long time in this position, he observed her face with the intense concentration of one who would draw it. At last, shaking her arm a little and nodding to himself three times in silent agreement with something, he made such a pitiful and deep sigh that it seemed capable of ending his life. He then let her go and went out of the room, but as he left his head was turned over his shoulder and he continued to stare at her until he was out of the door.

COMMENT

When last we saw Hamlet, his mind had been unsettled by his meeting with the Ghost, which raised further questions about the nature of this Ghost. Ophelia's comment that he now looked "as if he had been loosed out of hell to speak of horrors" strengthens the view even further that the Ghost has been playing a devilish role toward Hamlet both in his disclosures and commands, for Hamlet's soul now appears to be in the power of hell.

As this scene comes right after the scene with the Ghost and as nothing has yet been said about any passage of time, its dramatic effect upon the spectator is to reinforce the evidence of the Ghost scene. In Act III: Scene 2, Ophelia reveals that two months have passed since the events in Act I. But, as we shall see, when Ophelia says that it is "twice two months" since his father died, Hamlet replies, "die two months ago, and not forgotten yet?" This indicates that, for Hamlet, time has stopped since his encounter with the Ghost, for this occurred on the day when, in his first soliloquy, Hamlet had said that his father was "but two months dead, nay, not so much, not two."

In terms of Hamlet's psychology, then, as well as of dramatic effect, the scene with Ophelia seems to be a direct effect of his encounter with the Ghost. In despair over the Ghost's disclosures about his mother's incestuous adultery with his uncle, Hamlet comes to his beloved's room to search her face for some proof that she is not like his mother. As he searches her frightened face, he seems to find only confirmation for what he feared, as his nodding head and anguished sigh reveal. Furthermore, he has some justification for his disillusionment with her. As we immediately learn, Ophelia, following her father's orders, has rejected Hamlet's advances after having first been most obliging. Her face may look innocent, as it most assuredly does, but this only proves her falseness. Like his mother to his father, she can appear loving and then immediately change her behavior. As he looks so deeply into her eyes, he may perceive some potentiality for lust which nobody should suspect but which is later revealed by the sensual vulgarity she displays in her insanity. Finally, even in this scene she fails him, for she stands with mute terror at the sight of his anguish and does nothing to try to understand or calm him. The effect of this is to destroy whatever lingering love he may still have felt for her and to confirm his belief in the frailty of all women.

Polonius decides that Hamlet is suffering from frustrated love and, forgetful once more, asks Ophelia whether she has quarreled with him. She replies: "No, my good lord; but as you did command/I did repel his letters and denied/His access to me." Polonius, having forgotten all about his hasty command, concludes that this is the source of Hamlet's madness. He makes an unusual admission about his own character; he admits that he showed poor judgment with regards to Hamlet's intentions but excuses this on the grounds of old age: "By heaven, it is as proper to our age/To cast beyond ourselves in our opinions/As it is common for the younger sort/To lack discretion." Old age, he says, is given to authoritarian presumption of its wisdom while having lost the power of true judgment. He now decides to take Ophelia to the King with this discovery as to the source of Hamlet's madness.

SUMMARY

This scene accomplishes the following purposes:
1. It confirms our opinion of Polonius, showing him to be a foolish, authoritarian old man who yet prides himself on his power of intrigue. The scene begins with Polonius' instructions to Reynaldo as to how he should spy upon his son and ends with his going to Claudius with, as we shall see, new plans for spying. In both of these instances he shows no more respect or regard for his children's feelings than he did for Hamlet's. He is sending his servant to spy upon his son and violating his daughter's modesty and feelings by bringing her before the King in order to advance his own position in the King's respect, to prove to him that, despite his advancing age, he is just as good a counselor-of-state as he ever was under the late King Hamlet.
2. The narrated scene in Ophelia's room (called "closet" in Elizabethan times) serves three purposes:
a. It continues the thematic questioning of the Ghost's true identity, reinforcing the suspicion that it is actually a devil, since Hamlet's soul has been reduced to a state of hell.
b. It introduces through narration the change in Hamlet's behavior and attire before we actually see him. In Act I: Scene 2, we were told that Hamlet was dressed in complete mourning but there was nothing said of any disarray. Now we are told that his clothing is completely disordered and dirty. Critic John Dover Wilson suggests that this is

the way he is to dress for much of the remainder of the play: it is the sign of his assumed madness, though his emotional disturbance over Ophelia seems genuine enough.

c. It shows that Hamlet's continuing disturbance over the infidelity of his mother has now affected his ability to love Ophelia, and it marks his last moment of genuine involvement with her while she lives.

ACT II: SCENE 2

The scene shifts to a room in the castle where Claudius and Gertrude are greeting Rosencrantz and Guildenstern. These gentlemen are Hamlet's boyhood friends whom Claudius has called to Denmark in the hope that they may be able to help him investigate the nature of Hamlet's increasing mental disorder. His "transformation," earlier described by Ophelia, seems to Claudius to have resulted from more than simply his father's death, and Claudius hopes that by discovering the reason for this these friends may help him to restore Hamlet's health. The Queen seconds this with the promise of an ample reward, and the two men agree to help the King.

COMMENT

This scene indicates that some time has passed during which Hamlet's behavior has become increasingly mad. Whether Hamlet has achieved anything by this means we do not yet know, but we do know that it has caused speculation in the court and sufficient worry on Claudius' part for him to have sent for two spies to investigate Hamlet. Whereas earlier Claudius was anxious only to gain Hamlet's goodwill, Hamlet's "madness" has now placed Claudius on guard against him. Polonius' delight to have discovered, as he thinks, the cause of Hamlet's "madness" and his immediate going to Claudius with the news show how concerned the court and particularly Claudius had become with the topic of Hamlet's "madness."

Polonius enters with the news of the return of the ambassadors to Norway. He then says: "And I do think—or else this
brain of mine/Hunts not the trail of policy so sure/As it hath
used to do—that I have found/The very cause of Hamlet's
lunacy." If Polonius was forced in the last scene to admit that
his lack of judgment was a symptom of old age, he now hopes
to dispel any similar doubt that Claudius may have about his
continuing usefulness. Claudius is more anxious to hear of
this than of the results of his ambassadors: "O, speak of that!
That do I long to hear." Polonius asks that the ambassadors
be attended to first and Claudius agrees. While Polonius goes
to bring in the ambassadors, Claudius tells his "dear Gertrude"
that Polonius thinks he has discovered the source of her son's
disorder, but she is convinced that she already knows the
reason: "I doubt it is no other but the main/His father's death
and our o'erhasty marriage."

COMMENT

This private conference reveals two things about
Gertrude: she has good insight into her son's character
and lacks of any possible knowledge of her former
husband's murder. It is interesting that while Claudius
had only mentioned his father's death as a possible
reason for Hamlet's madness, Gertrude is also sensitive
to the effect her hasty remarriage has had upon her son.
Claudius' term of endearment toward her also indicates
that his feelings for her far exceed lust, as will be shown
more fully later on.

Voltemand enters with the news of his successful mission to
Norway. The King of Norway, upon investigating Fortinbras'
activities, had found Claudius to be correct and, very grieved
by this, had restrained his nephew from attacking Denmark.
He has, however, decided to deploy Fortinbras and the force
he has raised against Poland. He now asks Claudius' permission for the safe passage of these troops through Denmark on
their way to Poland. Claudius' immediate reaction to this is

positive but he is far too impatient to hear Polonius' theory about Hamlet to give his full attention to this matter now. Telling the ambassadors that they will feast together at night, he bids them retire now and turns to Polonius.

Although saying that "brevity is the soul of wit," Polonius is so long-winded about getting to the point that the Queen finally interrupts him with the words, "More matter, with less art." Nonetheless, Polonius continues awhile with comically pretentious rhetoric until he finally gets to the point: his daughter has obediently given him a love letter to her from Hamlet. He reads this letter aloud. It rivals his own comic speeches in its over-wrought, conventional love melancholy. Claudius, satisfied with Hamlet's love for Ophelia, asks Polonius how she has received his love. He replies that his duty toward the King led him to tell his daughter that, as the Prince was so far above her, "she should lock herself from his resort,/Admit no messengers, receive no tokens." She had done this and the result of this rejection of his love, Polonius concludes, has led to Hamlet's madness. Claudius asks Gertrude whether she thinks this is the reason, and she replies, "It may be, very like." Polonius claims that his advice has always been correct and that they should behead him "if this be otherwise."

Claudius asks him what they might do to further investigate his theory. Polonius suggests a plan which he had evidently prepared beforehand. He says that there is a place in the palace where Hamlet often walks for hours at a time. "At such a time I'll loose my daughter to him," he suggests, while the King and he observe from behind a hanging tapestry the nature of their encounter. If this does not prove his case, he concludes, "Let me be no assistant for a state/But keep a farm and carters." The King agrees to try Polonius' plan, whereupon Hamlet enters.

COMMENT

In *What Happens in Hamlet*, John Dover Wilson has

proposed the theory, which has recently gained wide-spread critical and theatrical acceptance, that Hamlet entered unobserved at the back of the stage before his announced entrance and thus overheard the plot. Such a theory seriously alters the usual reading of the altar scene, as shall be discussed at that time. Although Wilson argues his case very persuasively, it is by no means proven. A second point about this last portion of the scene is how Polonius becomes a comic figure, posturing ridiculously about both his verbal style and his subtle reasoning, though we may note a touch of increasing insecurity about his value to the state.

Speaking of Hamlet, the Queen notes how "sadly the poor wretch comes reading," and Polonius begs them to leave him alone with Hamlet. He tries to make conversation with Hamlet but Hamlet counters everything he says with apparently mad but actually quite satiric thrusts. He calls Polonius a "fishmonger," which also meant a pimp, and tells him that he had better not let his daughter walk in the sun as she may conceive spontaneously like maggots.

COMMENT

Wilson uses this to support his theory that Hamlet over-heard Polonius' conference with the King, since Polonius' statement to "loose" his daughter to him is language which an Elizabethan procurer would use in reference to his whore. In any case, Hamlet is speaking very coarsely about Ophelia.

Further convinced by this that Hamlet's madness has resulted from his disappointed love, Polonius now asks him what he is reading. After bandying about with this for a while. Hamlet finally says that he is reading slanders against old age by a "satirical rogue" who says that "old men have grey beards, that their faces are wrinkled" and "that they have a plentiful lack of wit, together with most weak hams," all of which, he agrees with, but he does not think it decent to write down since Polonius, himself, is old. At this Polonius silently comments, "Though this be madness, yet there is method in't." After a few more lines in which Hamlet shows a disconcerting wit, Polonius decides to leave and says, "I will most humbly take my leave of you." Hamlet begins to return this satirically but then his mood abruptly changes: "You cannot, sir, take from me anything that I will more willingly part withal—except my life, except my life, except my life." After Polonius starts to leave, Hamlet expresses his final disgust with Polonius: "These tedious old fools!"

COMMENT

This is the first glimpse we gain of Hamlet's supposed "madness." We see it takes the form of brilliant but savage satirical wit. Hamlet is using the mask of madness here as a license to say anything he feels like saying. From his own statement, we know that Hamlet feels Polonius to be a tedious old fool and has no use for him, but his role of madman permits him to make unmerciful fun of Polonius. Indeed, Hamlet here exhibits an extreme hatred and bitterness toward Polonius. This might be explained by Hamlet's awareness of Polonius' interference with his love and, possibly, Polonius' plan to use Ophelia against him in the service of his enemy, Claudius. Our respect for Polonius has been so reduced by this time, however, that we can hardly blame Hamlet for his treatment of him. In his last lines to Polonius moreover, we see that Hamlet is still in the same psychological state in which we first saw him, the rapid alternation between destructive satire and self-destructive melancholy, between hysteria and depression.

Rosencrantz and Guildenstern now enter. Hamlet happily greets them as "My excellent good friends!" After some introductory kidding with them about the state of their fortune, he asks them what they have done to deserve being sent here to "prison." When they question Hamlet's reference to Denmark as a prison, he replies: "Why, then 'tis none to you, for there is nothing either good or bad but thinking makes it so. To me it is a prison." Seizing this opportunity to begin their investigation, they suggest, "Why, then your ambition makes it one." After arguing this point, he asks them again, in the "way of friendship," what they are doing at Elsinore. They reply that they have come simply to visit him. Hamlet thanks them for this but then immediately asks whether it is a free visit or whether they were sent for by the King and Queen. They hesitate to answer him; he asks them again; and, as they finally confer on an answer, Hamlet says to himself, "Nay then, I have an eye of you." They finally do admit, "My, lord, we were sent for," but it is too late—they have alienated Hamlet's trust.

In one of the most beautiful speeches in the play, Hamlet explains to them why they were sent for: "I have of late—but wherefore I know not—lost all my mirth." In his depressed state, the good earth seems to him "a sterile promontory," the majestic heavens appear "nothing to him but a foul and pestilent congregation of vapors," man, himself, with his noble reason, infinite faculties and beauty, seems to him the "quintessence of dust."

COMMENT

Here, Hamlet explains the source of his statement that "there is nothing either good or bad but thinking makes it so," that our understanding of objective reality depends upon our perception of it which differs from individual to individual and from time to time. Although Hamlet's reason and memory tell him that the earth, heavens, and man are beautiful and meaningful, something in his spirit has made him no longer able to perceive them that way. Life and the heavens seem sterile and meaningless because humans can only come to dust. He does not know why he should feel this so deeply.

Although he counters their earlier suggestion, which evidently came from Claudius, that it is disappointed ambition, there is also about his words the tone of true confession. Throughout most of the play, Hamlet continues to try to analyze what has depressed him so deeply. Claudius and his followers also try to analyze Hamlet's condition, as we have seen. Finally, critics of the play for hundreds of years have tried to explain this central mystery at the heart of the play. Hamlet's statement here, then, is the starting point for the "problem of Hamlet."

Rosencrantz and Guildenstern tell Hamlet a company of actors is coming to Elsinore. There is some discussion between them about acting and acting companies. This discussion reflects the conditions in the Elizabethan theater at the time. Before the players enter, however, Hamlet tells Rosencrantz and Guildenstern that they are welcome to Elsinore. More than this, he also tells them that Claudius and Gertrude are deceived about his madness, that he is only mad when he feels like it and can otherwise be perfectly sane, as indeed has been shown in this scene with them.

COMMENT

Since Hamlet has already concluded that Rosencrantz and Guildenstern are spies, he is very careless in making this important admission to them. This can only be explained as forgetfulness on Hamlet's part due to his enjoyment of their company, to his ability to discuss with them such varied topics as the state of his soul and the condition of theatrical companies. This is one of the first signs of Hamlet's lack of precaution in his dealings with Claudius, as opposed to Claudius' many precautions throughout the play.

Polonius enters with the players. He introduces them with comical pretentiousness which leads Hamlet once again to assume the role of madman and to make fun of him. Hamlet welcomes the players. He asks them as a proof of their quality to recite a speech from one of their plays about the death of Priam, the old King of Troy, which he begins. Polonius praises Hamlet's delivery and one of the players continues the speech.

In the speech, Pyrrhus drives at Priam but "in rage strikes wide." Nonetheless, Priam, the "unnervèd father," falls from the wind of Pyrrhus' sword. Instead of killing him then, however, "his sword,/Which was declining on the milky head/Of reverend Priam, seemed i' th' air to stick" and, against his own will, "did nothing." Finally, however, "arousèd vengeance sets him new awork" and never did blows fall like those now on Priam. The player continues with an impassioned speech on Hecuba's grief over the death of her husband, Priam. Hamlet is delighted with the player's recitation and asks him whether the company could play "The Murder of Gonzago" that night with an insertion of a speech of "some dozen or sixteen lines" which he would write himself. The player agrees to do this and Hamlet tells Polonius to see that the players are well looked after, upon which they all depart, leaving Hamlet alone.

COMMENT

The speech that Hamlet remembers and wants to hear recited is interesting as a reflection of Hamlet's own preoccupations. In the speech a revenger is at first unable to commit revenge, but can only act wildly. This, however, disarms his opponent and eventually he is able to accomplish his revenge with great vigor. The situation parallels Hamlet's own plight.

Months have passed and instead of sweeping to his revenge as he had told the Ghost he would do, Hamlet has only acted madly. That he is beginning to feel some guilt about his delay is shown by his remembrance of this speech with its similar delay in achieving revenge. Hamlet hopes to quiet his conscience by remembering that a similar revenger finally did accomplish his purposes, but the guilt only further emerges when he is alone.

We now come to Hamlet's second soliloquy. Hamlet begins with the exclamation: "O, what a rogue and peasant slave am I!" It seems monstrous to him that the player could so work himself up "for nothing,/For Hecuba!/What's Hecuba to him, or he to Hecuba,/That he should weep for her?" He wonders "what would he do/Had he the motive and the cue for passion/That I have?" Though the player, with such real motivation would "make mad the guilty," he, "a dull and muddy-mettled rascal," moans about in a dream without any real feeling for his cause and "can say nothing," no, not even for a dear King who was cursedly murdered. He asks himself whether he is a "coward." At first he is horrified by such a humiliating suggestion, but then he concedes that it must be so, that "I am pigeon-livered and lack gall/To make oppression bitter" since he has not yet fattened the vultures with Claudius' guts. He tries to work up a passion against Claudius by yelling: "Bloody, bawdy villain!/Remorseless, treacherous, lecherous, kindless villain!/O, vengeance!" But then he immediately realizes, "Why, what an ass am I!" This is some bravery, that the son of a dear murdered father, "prompted to my revenge by heaven and hell," must release his feelings simply with words rather than with action.

Hamlet puts his brains to work upon the revenge. He remembers having heard "that guilty creatures sitting at a play" which represented their own crime have been so struck by guilt that they have confessed their crime. He decides (apparently having already forgotten that he had just instructed the players to do the same thing) that he will "have these players/Play something like the murder of my father/Before mine uncle. I'll observe his looks" and if he but flinches "I know my course." This is the first time we have seen Hamlet express any doubt about his course, but the reason he gives is one that he may well have entertained:

> The spirit that I have seen
> May be a devil, and the devil hath power

T'assume a pleasing shape, yea, and perhaps
Out of my weakness and my melancholy,
As he is very potent with such spirits,
Abuses me to damn me.

He decides that he needs further objective proof of Claudius'
guilt and that "The play's the thing/Wherein I'll catch the conscience of the king."

COMMENT

The second soliloquy shows us the following important
things about Hamlet:

1. Hamlet has not been able to concentrate on the
subject of his revenge for reasons that he cannot understand. When a chance circumstance does cause him to
think about it, he feels guilty. This causes him to rationalize about his delay. Not that his suspicion about the
Ghost is not valid, but it is an after-thought to explain
his delay, rather than its actual cause.

2. We see, however, that when Hamlet does think about
his revenge he is caught up in a conflict of values. This
is a conflict between the honor code and the religious
code. The honor code distinguished the aristocrat from
the "peasant slave." His "gall" was quickly raised by any
sign of "oppression" or humiliation and he was always
ready to bravely risk his life to vindicate his honor or
the honor of his family. One of the obligations of a man
of honor was to revenge the death of his father; not to
do this was to be a "coward," the mark of the "peasant
slave" who desired only to preserve his life whatever
the cost. When, however, dishonor was inevitable, the
honor code preached suicide as the only way of prov-
ing one's superiority to his fate. The man of honor
aspired to greatness and was only afraid of shame.

In contrast to this, the religious code preached that
goodness was superior to greatness. Goodness ex-

presses itself not through a vaunting superiority to fate but a humble acceptance of whatever heaven may send. As Job says in the Bible, "The Lord giveth and the Lord taketh away. Blessed be the name of the Lord." As a Christian gentleman, Hamlet is pulled by both of these opposing codes of values. He cannot bear the thought of dishonor, though the vindication of his honor and nobility can only be accomplished through murder, and he is also anxious to secure the salvation of his soul which premeditated murder would place in danger of damnation. The "Christian gentleman" was a contradiction in terms since such a character desired to avoid both shame in this world and damnation in the next and he could not have it both ways.

3. If this conflict in values is not the primary cause of Hamlet's delay and mental disorder, it is of primary thematic importance for the play, for it is by these codes that we are asked to evaluate Hamlet. Thus it is the spectator as well as Hamlet who must decide which of these codes is to be preferred. It is also in terms of this question that the Ghost is to be judged. If the Ghost is demanding of Hamlet that which will damn him, and if the question of salvation is more important than that of honor, then the spectator should seriously consider with Hamlet the possibility that the Ghost may be a devil who has been attracted by his melancholy to tempt him into a damnable murder. It may well be, then, that Hamlet is ethically right to delay his revenge even though the question of ethics is not the primary source of delay.

SUMMARY

This scene accomplishes the following purposes:

1. It shows Hamlet's assumed madness in both words and behavior and theorizes as to its source: Polonius believes it comes from disappointed love; Rosencrantz and Guildenstern, probably from a cue by Claudius, believe it results from frus-

trated ambition for the throne; Gertrude believes it results simply from Hamlet's shock at the death of his father and her hasty remarriage; and Hamlet is at a loss to explain the drastic inner change that has come over him.

2. It begins the chief characters' cross-plotting against each other. Hamlet's assumed madness, which was supposed to achieve some unspecified and probably unthought of purpose, has now so raised Claudius' suspicions that he has sent Rosencrantz and Guildenstern to spy upon Hamlet, which they begin to do in this scene. Polonius plans to test his theory by confronting Hamlet with his daughter while Claudius and he spy upon the meeting from behind a tapestry. Hamlet plans to test the Ghost's truth and Claudius' guilt through a play upon a similar crime which he will revise for this purpose. These last two plots occupy much of the first two scenes of Act III.

3. It further exhibits Hamlet's character, his savage wit toward Polonius, his profound reflective quality in conversation with Rosencrantz and Guildenstern, his delight to see them and the players, his love of the theater, and his savage attack upon himself, combined with his lack of personal understanding.

HAMLET
ACT III

ACT III: SCENE 1

The scene is set in the room in the castle where the encounter between Hamlet and Ophelia is to take place. The King, Queen, Polonius, Ophelia, Rosencrantz, Guildenstern, and others are present. Claudius is asking Rosencrantz and Guildenstern whether they have discovered anything concerning the cause of Hamlet's madness, but they answer that Hamlet "with a crafty madness" has kept from "confession of his true state." Gertrude asks them how Hamlet received them and whether they have been able to interest him in any pastime. They reply that he treated them like a gentleman and was over-joyed by their news of the arrival of a company of players whom he has already ordered to appear this night. Polonius says that Hamlet has asked the King and Queen to attend the performance, and Claudius says that he is happy to hear of Hamlet's new interest and will support it by going to the play.

Rosencrantz and Guildenstern leave. Claudius suggests that Gertrude also leave as he has sent for Hamlet that he may accidentally meet Ophelia. Claudius and Polonius will spy on the encounter to test whether Polonius is correct when he claims that Hamlet's madness comes from disappointed love. Gertrude tells Ophelia that she hopes Ophelia is "the happy cause of Hamlet's madness" and that, if her virtues are able to cure him, there would be a hope for their marriage. As Ophelia seconds her hope, Gertrude leaves. Polonius instructs Ophelia that she is to walk there by herself reading a pious book. This would serve to explain her lonely presence. He now reflects, as well he might, that people are often to blame for covering evil behavior with a show of "pious action." In an "aside" (a speech spoken to the audience and meant to indicate silent thought), Claudius reveals that Polonius' words have stung his conscience, for he too covers his deed with behavior as false as a harlot's painted charms. Keeping this lie a secret has become so difficult for him that he cries out, "O heavy burden!"

COMMENT

This is the first objective proof we have had to substantiate the Ghost's charges against Claudius, for he admits an unspecified evil "deed." In this admission, furthermore, we see that Claudius does have an essentially moral nature, for his conscience can become anguished by a chance remark. This also prepares us for Claudius' hysterical breakdown during the performance of the play in the next scene. All of this shows us that Claudius is not naturally evil and is oppressed both by the guilt of having committed evil and by the falseness he has to assume to cover the fact of his guilt.

As Hamlet approaches, Claudius and Polonius withdraw behind the painted tapestry to watch his encounter with Ophelia.

Hamlet is so involved with his own thoughts that he does not at first see Ophelia. He delivers the famous "To be or not to be" soliloquy. He begins by questioning which is the "nobler" code of behavior, that which bids one "to be," to live even though this means "to suffer" from "outrageous fortune," or that which bids one "not to be," to commit suicide and thus "end" one's suffering through the act of "opposing" the outrage which fortune would do him. "To die," he reasons, is "to sleep—no more," and by such a sleep it is possible to "end the heartache, and the thousand natural shocks" that human beings inherit in the process of being born. Such an end to human troubles, he concludes, is "a consummation devoutly to be wished." "To die," he repeats, is "to sleep," but in sleep, he now remembers, there is also the possibility of dreams and this creates a new difficulty. For when we have cast off the difficulties of life "in that sleep of death," we do not know "what dreams may come," and this must cause us to hesitate before committing suicide. This is what causes people to endure the "calamity" of a "long life." For who would bear the injuries of existence, the wrongs and humiliations of oppression, "the pangs of despised love," the delay in both law and position which those with merit must patiently bear from the unworthy and insolent people who do receive high office, who would bear the general burdens of "a weary life,"

> But that the dread of something after death,
> The undiscovered country, from whose bourn
>   [confinement]
> No traveler returns, puzzles the will,
> And makes us rather bear those ills we have
> Than fly to others that we know not of?

This awareness of the religious problem involved with suicide, the dread of eternal punishment, "does make cowards of us all," and "the pale cast of thought" sickens the power of "resolution." This not only with regards to suicide but to all great "enterprises," whose force is similarly turned away into inaction through overconsideration. He now sees Ophelia at her prayers and tells her to include in them "all my sins."

COMMENT

During the "rogue and peasant slave" soliloquy, we saw Hamlet feeling guilty over his long inaction. This was resolved by a new commitment to a course of positive action. Now, but a few hours later, we see him sunk once more in suicidal melancholy, forgetful of the whole question of revenge. He is, however, still concerned by the conflict between the honor and religious codes, but it is now centered on the question of suicide rather than murder. As either course would lead him into mortal sin, he does well to tell Ophelia to pray for "all my sins." Though prompted by honor first to revenge and now to suicide, his religious beliefs inhibit him from taking such action.

But the power of his religion over him is more negative than positive; it is fear of eternal punishment rather than the value of righteousness which motivates him. As fear, however, is an ignoble emotion, his sense of honor arises once more to accuse him of cowardice, just as it did in the previous soliloquy. He concludes that the reason for the cowardly inaction which he despises in himself is that he overintellectualizes his problems to the point of inertia. Hamlet's conclusion here has been accepted by the great nineteenth-century English poet and critic, Samuel Taylor Coleridge, as the solution to the problem of Hamlet's inactivity. It has remained one of the standard critical approaches to the play although it is less in favor at present.

We see that as long as the power of Hamlet's religion over him is a negative one, it cannot destroy the influence of the honor code upon his spirit, but simply inhibits its power to motivate sustained positive action. Hamlet remains a prey to the worst effects of both codes, guilt and shame, which has the additional result of driving him still further into suicidal melancholy. Just thinking of taking action so overwhelms him with internal conflicts that he wants to kill himself, as we see in the third soliloquy. But this in turn produces its own vicious cycle of guilt, followed by shame. This proceeds to such a point that he feels shackled by his very consciousness of such thoughts, and blames them in turn for his inactivity.

His conflicts, rather than any overintellectualizing, produce his inertia. The inertia is there; the intellectualizing comes after as an attempt to understand the inactivity. It then becomes useful to Hamlet as a means of rationalizing his unfathomed apathy and melancholy. As we have seen in the two past soliloquies, Hamlet thinks about his problems just when he can develop some rationalization for his inactivity. In the second soliloquy it is doubt about the Ghost's nature; in the third soliloquy it is overintellectualization of his problems. Then he concludes his inner investigations, fully satisfied for the time.

One other interesting statement he makes here is that "no traveler returns" from "the undiscovered country" of death. Such a statement would deny that the Ghost was the spirit of his father returned from death. It would also indicate that his doubt about the Ghost had grown stronger in the interval between the two soliloquies. This in turn would free him from the sense of obligation to commit revenge, and so the necessity for life, and enable him more freely to contemplate suicide. But this statement also indicates a weakening of his religious convictions to a point of agnosticism, further showing the negative quality of his religion and perhaps even a result of the ever more deadening effect of religious commandments upon his impulses. This agnosticism, however, is important for tragedy which requires the spectator to feel that death is dreadful. If there were no question that Hamlet was going to heaven at the end of the play (as Horatio claims), his death would not really be tragic.

One final question concerns the form of this soliloquy. There are some modern critics who see it only as an exercise in rhetoric such as Hamlet might have studied at the University of Wittenberg. While it is true that the question form of the soliloquy, with the balancing of two alternatives, is similar to rhetorical exercises of the time and might indicate that Hamlet was using his logical training to attack his personal problems, to dismiss the whole soliloquy as an intellectual exercise or game is going too far, for the first soliloquy is also personally concerned with suicide and Hamlet is immediately to make some further suicidal statements in his scene with Ophelia.

The meeting between Hamlet and Ophelia begins politely as Ophelia asks Hamlet how he has been feeling these past days and he replies that he has been feeling well. She then tells him that she has with her some things he had given her which she has long wanted to return to him. She prays him now to receive them. He denies having given her anything and she, apparently hurt by this, says that she knows very well that he did and with his presents added such sweet words "as made the things more rich." Since this sweetness is now gone, she bids him take back his presents, for "rich gifts wax poor when givers prove unkind."

He laughs hysterically and asks her whether she is "honest," and again whether she is "fair" (that is, "white" as is the color of purity and virtue). She does not understand what he is driving at and asks him what he means. He answers, "That if you be honest and fair, your honesty should admit no discourse to your beauty," that is, if she were truly virtuous, she would not admit anyone to approach her beauty. She takes his verbal quibble in another sense and asks him whether beauty could do better than to go with honesty. He becomes more hysterical and says that she is right, for beauty has such power that it can "transform honesty from what it is to a bawd." He then abruptly claims, "I did love you once." She, still hurt though now apparently vindicated, answers, "Indeed, my lord, you made me believe so." To this Hamlet lashes out at her that she should not have believed him since his stock is so sullied that it is incapable of virtue. He abruptly claims, "I loved you not," and she even more sadly replies, "I was the more sadly deceived." He cries out to her in a long, bitter speech:

> Get thee to a nunnery. Why wouldest thou be a breeder of sinners? I am myself indifferent honest, but yet I could accuse me of such things that it were better my mother had not borne me: I am very proud, revengeful, ambitious, with more offenses at my beck than I have thoughts

to put them in, imagination to give them shape, or time to act them in. What should such fellows as I do crawling between earth and heaven? We are arrant knaves all; believe none of us. Go thy ways to a nunnery.

He asks her where her father is. When she replies that he is at home, he says that Polonius should be locked in there "that he may play the fool nowhere but in's own house." He bids her "farewell," but, as she prays to heaven to help him, he continues that if she should marry she can take this curse with her: however chastely she may behave she will still gain a bad reputation. He tells her again to go to a nunnery, says farewell again, and then continues that if she must marry she should marry a fool, "for wise men know well enough what monsters you make of them." He sends her to a nunnery again and says farewell again.

As she prays again to heaven to restore his sanity, he continues his outburst against her, this time directed against women's cosmetics, "paintings." He charges, "God hath given you one face, and you make yourselves another." As he continues railing against women's seductive movements, tones, and nicknaming habits, he finally cries out, "Go to, I'll no more on't; it hath made me mad." He demands that there be no more marriages, though, "all but one" of those who are married "shall live." He tells her to go to a nunnery a final time and leaves without another word. Ophelia is in a state of shocked despair at her former lover's behavior. In a return to poetry after the prose of the last section, she exclaims, "O, what a noble mind is here o'erthrown!" He who was the ideal courtier, soldier, and scholar, the hope of the state, the model of fashion and manners, and of a most noble intelligence, is now completely disordered by madness. She, who received the sweetness of his love, is the most wretched of ladies.

COMMENT

Ophelia acts as though she were the injured party though

we know it was she who first rejected Hamlet. His amazed question as to whether she is being honest or hypocritical is natural enough. Though her sense of injury may have come from their last, silent meeting (which she recounted to her father) in which Hamlet did, indeed, reject her, she seems to have little understanding then as now of her own responsibility for his present behavior toward her. Hamlet's suspicions toward her may have been aroused not only by her assumption of innocence but also by her presence, fully prepared with all the things he had given her, at a place to which he was summoned. His belief that she is being a hypocrite may be even further explained by the theory that he overheard the plan for this meeting and is now remembering this.

Regardless, he begins to play a part of his own with her, assuming once more his role of madman. But the savagery of his attack on her and the nature of his disclosures about himself indicate that it may not be all an act, that his mind has been truly unsettled behind its assumed madness by this new "proof" of the falseness of the woman he once loved.

This proof further supports the generalization he had made about his mother, "frailty, thy name is woman." In his continuing attacks he identifies Ophelia more and more with his mother. As he thinks about his mother's lustful nature, however, he begins to doubt his own feelings, since he is her son and has inherited a debased nature from her which may be incapable of any higher feeling than lust. If his own feelings for Ophelia could not be trusted, neither can any other man's and it were better for Ophelia to leave the world of dishonest men and get to a nunnery. Not only should she not continue the process of breeding sinners, but neither should anyone else; there should be no more marriages, no more sex. Some critics, following John Dover Wilson, argue that since the term "nunnery" was used in Elizabethan slang to refer to brothels, Hamlet is actually suggesting the opposite of what he appears to be saying, namely, that since she is playing the false part of the harlot with him she may as well drop any pretense of virtue and become a professional whore. This view is further strengthened by Wilson's theory that Hamlet overheard Polonius' slang references to his daughter as a whore, now recognizes that she is being used by her father, and is directing this to Polonius' ears as well.

We have already touched on the second important item, Hamlet's attitude toward himself. We remember that just before the start of this scene, upon seeing "the fair Ophelia," he had asked her to remember his sins in her prayers. Now he says that he could accuse himself "of such things that it were better my mother had not borne me," not only the things which are present to his conscious mind but offenses which he cannot even put into thought. As he thinks about his mother's whore-like falseness and the falseness of Ophelia, with their "paintings" and seductive ways, he cries out for an end to sex, for "it hath made me mad."

This suggests that Hamlet is revolted by his mother's sensuality. The thought that he may have inherited her nature and may be capable of equally base sexual desires is more than he can bear. The famous psychoanalyst Ernest Jones has suggested that Hamlet had an "Oedipus Complex." Freudian theory states that at a certain stage of their development, all men subconsciously desire to reenact the crimes of the mythical Greek King, Oedipus, who murdered his father and married his mother. Hamlet had repressed these forbidden desires and grown up into a model young man. When Hamlet learns that Claudius has murdered Hamlet's father and married his mother, his "Oedipus Complex" is reactivated though still repressed, because his conscious mind cannot accept his feelings. Therefore, he feels suicidally revolted with himself for reasons that he cannot fathom. Moreover, he is subconsciously unable to condemn Claudius for having committed the very crimes he himself desired subconsciously to commit. But since he is not consciously aware of his "Oedipus Complex," he is at a loss to understand the source of his inability to act or even to think in any sustained fashion of such action.

Another explanation of this scene is based on the theory that Hamlet overheard the plot to test him with Ophelia and that he is here acting a mad role primarily for the benefit of Claudius and Polonius. Thus he justifies Claudius' theory while at the same time warning him that "all but one shall live," and justifies Polonius' theory that it is women's false love which "hath made me mad." At the same time, he can directly attack Polonius as a fool and father of a whore.

Ophelia's closing description of Hamlet describes him as he was before his father's death and his mother's remarriage, which had already affected his mind at the beginning of the play.

Claudius and Polonius now come out from their hiding place. Each is convinced of the truth of his own theory as to Hamlet's condition. Claudius begins by rejecting Polonius' theory about love. He also notes that "what he [Hamlet] spake, though it lacked form a little,/Was not like madness." Claudius believes that there is something in Hamlet's soul which is causing him to brood and which will finally "hatch" into some "danger." To prevent this eventuality, Claudius immediately decides to send Hamlet "with speed to England" with the covering excuse that he will be going to demand of England the tribute it owes to Denmark. Claudius tells Polonius that he hopes the change of surroundings "shall expel/This something-settled matter in his heart," and asks Polonius what he thinks of the plan. Polonius agrees to it though he still believes "The origin and commencement of his grief/Sprung from neglected love."

Polonius asks Ophelia how she is but immediately turns from her to continue his discussion with Claudius despite his daughter's grief. Polonius suggests a new spying plan to Claudius. After the play, Gertrude should send for Hamlet and ask him to come alone to her room. She should then ask Hamlet plainly to explain to her what is troubling him. Polonius will hide in the room to overhear their conference. If Gertrude does not discover the source of Hamlet's melancholy, then Claudius should send Hamlet to England. Claudius agrees with Polonius' new plan, concluding "Madness in great ones must not unwatched go." They leave and the scene ends.

SUMMARY

This scene again contrasts the characters of Claudius and Hamlet as follows:

1. Claudius actively investigates Hamlet's disturbing behavior, first with Rosencrantz and Guildenstern and then with Ophelia. Though he discovers nothing definite, Hamlet's behavior with Ophelia is so threatening to him that he decides to send Hamlet to England and thus protect himself. Claudius is a man of practical action who does what is necessary to achieve his goals. Although Claudius will murder to gain a selfish end, he is not thoroughly evil. He feels genuine remorse for what he has done. He wants things to remain as they were at the beginning of the play so that he will not be forced to commit further evil acts.

2. Hamlet, on the other hand, is still incapable of action. Although he had recently decided on a plan of attack, now he has returned to suicidal melancholy. His scene with Ophelia brings out the worst aspect of his character, the almost inhuman savagery he shows to anyone he feels has injured him.

His savagery, however, is verbal. Ironically, no matter how Hamlet may threaten Claudius, he simply places himself at a greater disadvantage with regard to its object.

ACT III: SCENE 2

Hamlet tells the players how they are to perform. They are to pronounce the words easily rather than mouth them broadly and they are not to "saw the air too much" with their hands "but use all gently." Further, their passion should be controlled and smooth, for it is offensive to hear a "fellow tear a passion to tatters, to very rags, to split the ears of the groundlings, who for the most part are capable of nothing but inexplicable dumb shows and noise." But neither should they be too tame. He tells the actors to "suit the action to the word, the word to the action, with this special observance, that you o'erstep not the modesty of nature," for the purpose of drama from its origin to the present "was and is, to hold, as 'twere, the mirror up to nature." Though overacting may cause the uneducated to laugh, it "cannot but make the judicious grieve," and one of these outweighs a whole theater of the others. He has seen actors who "have so strutted and bellowed that I have thought some of Nature's journeymen had made men, and not made them well, they imitated humanity so abominably." The clowns should "speak no more than is set down for them" so that they do not obscure "some necessary question of the play" through the laughter of "barren spectators." The players agree and leave to prepare themselves for the performance.

COMMENT

This speech is generally seen as Shakespeare's own ideas on acting. He favored a more naturalistic form of acting than was practiced in his day. This is in line with the theory of drama he inherited from Aristotle which held that "tragedy is an imitation of an action and of life," that is, that it should be true to life. Shakespeare also felt that the play is more important than the performers, and that the few judicious observers who can understand the play are the playwright's real concern rather than a theater full of "barren spectators" who simply come to be entertained.

Polonius, Rosencrantz, and Guildenstern enter to tell Hamlet that the King and Queen will attend the performance, and Hamlet sends them out again to hurry the royal couple.

Hamlet tells Horatio that he considers him the most just man he has ever met. As a result, Hamlet has chosen Horatio to be his truest friend. It is Horatio's Stoicism which most attracts him:

> . . . for thou hast been/As one in suff'ring all that suffers nothing,/A man that Fortune's buffets and rewards/Hast ta'en with equal thanks; and blest are those/Whose blood and judgment are so well commeddled/That they are not a pipe for Fortune's finger/To sound what stop she please. Give me that man/That is not passion's slave, and I will wear him/In my heart's core, ay, in my heart of heart,/As I do thee.

COMMENT

It is clear that Hamlet is attracted to Horatio because Horatio represents opposite qualities from Hamlet. Hamlet is "passion's slave," an instrument for "Fortune's finger" to play upon as "she please." He cannot help but admire a person like Horatio who can accept Fortune's blows without suffering. He considers this a blessed condition and hopes that Horatio's presence may help him to control his own nature.

Hamlet reveals that he had earlier confided in Horatio about the circumstances of his father's death. He now continues this by confiding in Horatio his plan about the play soon to be performed. He asks Horatio to help him observe the way Claudius reacts to the part of the play which reenacts his crime and then to compare these observations with his own. He concludes that if Claudius' guilt does not reveal itself under these circumstances then "It is a damnèd Ghost that we have seen,/And my imaginations are as foul/As Vulcan's stithy [smithy]." Horatio agrees and, as the court is now approaching, he tells Horatio to part from him as he must now be "idle." This may refer to resuming a madman's role.

The King and court enter with a flourish of trumpets and drums. Claudius asks Hamlet how he is and Hamlet answers somewhat obscurely that he is not satisfied with eating promises (a suggestion of his disappointed ambition), but Claudius says he cannot make sense of what he is saying. Hamlet turns to Polonius and asks him about his university acting. Polonius says that he once played Julius Caesar and was killed in the Capitol. (This remark serves as a dramatic foreshadowing of Polonius' fate in the next scene.)

The players are now ready to appear and Gertrude asks Hamlet to sit by her. He rejects her, however, saying he prefers the more attractive Ophelia. This supports Polonius' theory, as Polonius quickly points out to Claudius. Hamlet lies at Ophelia's feet but he treats her without respect, making several lewd sexual puns (particularly one on "country matters" in which a pun is intended on the first syllable of "country"). These, however, seem to escape Ophelia's understanding. She notes simply that he is "merry." Hamlet replies: "O god, your only jig-maker! What should a man do but be merry?" Since God's creation is a farce, man can do nothing better than to laugh. Both of these points are proven by his mother's behavior: "For look you how cheerfully my mother looks, and my father died within's two hours." When Ophelia objects that " 'tis twice two months, my lord," Hamlet ironically returns, "O heavens! die two months ago, and not forgotten yet? Then there's hope a great man's memory may outlive his life half a year."

At this point the players put on the "dumb show," silently enacting the plot of the play: a king and queen embrace lovingly, then he lies down in a garden and she leaves. Another man comes in, takes off his crown and kisses it, pours poison in the sleeper's ear, and leaves him. The Queen returns, discovers that the King is dead, and displays passionate grief. The poisoner returns with some others and they try to comfort her. When the body is carried out, the poisoner woos the Queen, who, after some harshness, accepts his love.

COMMENT

The question arises as to why Claudius does not react to this clear demonstration of his crime. W. W. Greg first suggested that this proves Claudius is innocent of the specific crime the Ghost recounted to Hamlet. It also disproves the Ghost's validity. John Dover Wilson suggests that Claudius was probably still arguing with Polonius about the significance of Hamlet sitting with Ophelia and so did not notice the rapidly performed dumb show. Wilson also argues that Hamlet did not order the dumb show and that he was angered by it, but that it fortunately did no harm. As with Wilson's other theory of the "overheard plot," this makes good dramatic sense though without any textual support. Grebanier suggests that Claudius did recognize the similarity, but with strength of mind, rejected it as a coincidence.

The Player King and Player Queen begin the play. The play's major emphasis is the Queen's infidelity. The King begins by remembering how long they have been married and the Queen hopes they may continue married just as long, though she is very worried by his recent sickness. He replies that he shall not live long and hopes that she may find as kind a husband as he has been after he dies. She interrupts him, horrified by such a treasonous thought: "In second husband let me be accurst!/None wed the second but who killed the first."

In a long reply, the King says that though she may feel that way now, such purposes "like fruit unripe sticks on the tree,/ But fall unshaken when they mellow be." In time many things may change her present purposes. He concludes: "Our thoughts are ours, their ends none of our own." Nonetheless, the Queen makes a powerful vow that she will never remarry, and Hamlet exclaims: "If she should break it now!" He then asks his mother how she likes the play and Gertrude replies: "The lady doth protest too much, methinks." She seems quite innocent of Hamlet's more serious charge against her in the play, complicity in the murder.

Apparently aroused by the connection between the Player Queen and Gertrude, Claudius asks Hamlet whether he knows the plot of the play and whether there is any offense in it. Hamlet answers that there is "no offense i' th' world," and says the play is called "The Mousetrap." We remember that he had said, "The play's the thing/Wherein I'll catch the conscience of the King." Hamlet continues to play his cat-and-mouse game with Claudius by saying that the play is the story of a murder committed in Vienna. He then continues: " 'Tis a knavish piece of work, but what o' that? Your majesty, and we that have free souls, it touches us not." The Player Murderer enters and Hamlet announces that it is "Lucianus, nephew to the king." When Ophelia comments that he is as good as a stage narrator of the action, Hamlet turns to her and continues his earlier sexual joking with her. He finally calls to the actor playing Lucianus and tells him to begin. Lucianus approaches the sleeping Player King and carefully describes the properties of the poison he is to use. As Lucianus pours the poison in the Player King's ear, Hamlet once again starts to explain the story, but Claudius has already risen. Claudius is in a fury. He calls for more light and quickly leaves the hall, followed by everyone except Hamlet and Horatio.

Hamlet reacts to Claudius' breakdown with hysterical glee. He begins to sing and asks Horatio whether this play would not win him a share in a company of players. Horatio calmly answers that he would only earn "half a share," which Hamlet heartily disputes, and then he continues to sing. As he ends the verse poorly, Horatio again calmly notes, "You might have rhymed." This finally dampens Hamlet's high spirits long enough for him to discuss Claudius' reaction with Horatio and to conclude, "I'll take the Ghost's word for a thousand pound."

COMMENT

Although Hamlet had earlier said that he would write only one speech of twelve to sixteen lines, at the end of the performance he claims authorship for the whole scene. There is much about the scene which points to Hamlet's authorship. First, it displays greater preoccupation with the Queen's infidelity than with the King's murder. Second, it seems designed to catch his mother's conscience as well as Claudius' conscience. Despite the Ghost's warning, Hamlet, as we shall later see, suspects his mother knows about the murder and wishes to test her, a test she passes very well.

The King's long speech about "ripeness" and the contrary relationship of will to fate contains ideas which Hamlet is later to embrace as the explanation for his experiences. This speech may represent Hamlet's early testing of these ideas before he is fully ready to affirm them. The relationship of murderer to victim, as Wilson noted, is significantly changed from that of brother to nephew. As this is Hamlet's relationship to Claudius, rather than Claudius' relationship to his brother, the play serves to warn Claudius of Hamlet's intentions. This is the meaning which the rest of the court derives from the play, as we shall see in the next scene, and may even explain Claudius' disturbance. Therefore, it may still not prove the Ghost's story.

Hamlet's reaction to the play is so triumphant, however, as to suggest something further. Jones pointed out that as a playwright Hamlet has already accomplished his revenge vicariously through an artistic creation which substituted for reality. We have seen that Hamlet characteristically releases his destructive impulses through verbal play.

In continued high spirits, Hamlet calls for some music, asking the players to bring in the recorders, simple flute-like instruments. At this point Rosencrantz and Guildenstern enter and desire to talk with Hamlet. They tell Hamlet that the King is extremely upset. As Hamlet jokes about this with great gaiety, Guildenstern urges him to calm down: "Good my lord, put your discourse into some frame, and start not so wildly from my affair." Hamlet becomes calmer and Guildenstern continues his message, that Hamlet's mother "in most great affliction of spirit" has asked him to come to her room to speak with her before he goes to sleep. Hamlet interrupts this message several times until even he apologizes that he cannot make "a wholesome answer; my wit's deceased."

Rosencrantz asks Hamlet to open his heart to him and tell him the cause of his diseased mind. Hamlet quickly returns the answer Rosencrantz has been fishing for in their earlier meeting: "Sir, I lack advancement." When Rosencrantz asks how that can be since he has "the voice of the King himself for your succession in Denmark," Hamlet replies with half a proverb which obscurely intimates dissatisfaction with a long delay. A player enters with the recorders and Hamlet takes one. He now asks his friends why they are trying to catch him into a snare. Guildenstern objects that it is just the result of excessive love. Hamlet then asks Guildenstern to play the recorder for him. Guildenstern says he is unable to play the instrument because he does not know how. After repeated entreaties, Hamlet finally says:

Why, look you now, how unworthy a thing you make of me! You would play upon me, you would seem to know my stops, you would pluck out the heart of my mystery, you would sound me from my lowest note to the top of my compass; and there is much music, excellent voice, in this little organ, yet cannot you make it speak.

Polonius enters to tell Hamlet again that his mother wishes to speak to him at once. Hamlet, however, proceeds to have fun at Polonius' expense. He asks Polonius whether he sees a cloud shaped like a camel. When Polonius agrees, Hamlet changes his mind and says he thinks it looks first like a weasel and then like a whale. Polonius agrees each time. Finally, he tells Polonius that he will come to his mother soon. In an "aside" he says, "They fool me to the top of my bent," and then asks them all to leave him.

COMMENT

After the play Hamlet is genuinely unsettled, as Guildenstern points out. Hamlet agrees, but then he consciously puts on his mad pose for Polonius. He is finally tired of all of them and their hypocritical attempts to fool him. Although he despises them for their attempts to "pluck out the heart of my mystery," he is no closer to understanding the real cause of his diseased mind than they are.

Worn out by all the "fooling" with Rosencrantz, Guildenstern, and Polonius and commanded to see his mother, Hamlet's mood changes. Left alone in depressed spirits after his recent hysteria, he notes:

'Tis now the very witching time of night,/When churchyards yawn, and hell itself breathes out/Contagion to this world. Now could I drink hot blood/And do such bitter business as the day/Would quake to look on.

As he is going in this murderous mood to visit his mother, he tells his heart not to lose its natural feelings for her however cruelly he may act: "I will speak daggers to her, but use none." He then exits.

COMMENT

It is interesting that Hamlet is in a murderous mood before he visits his mother, even though she has been proven innocent. He sees such murderous impulses in the context of "hell" and the contagious disease it spreads. When Hamlet believes the Ghost to have been vindicated by his play, his mind becomes diseased and he feels himself to be in the power of hell. His primary concern at this point is to keep himself from murdering his mother; he seems to have completely forgotten about Claudius.

SUMMARY

Hamlet dominates this scene and reveals the following things about himself:

1. His understanding, love, and talent for the theater are shown by his advice to the players, the play he writes, and his delight with the performance.

2. He seems to be enjoying the game of espionage that he and everyone else is playing: he tests his mother as well as Claudius, bringing Horatio in to help him with the latter. He also throws out clues to everyone interested in the cause of his own disorder—he suggests to Claudius that the cause is frustrated ambition, and he arouses Polonius and perhaps his mother through his exhibitionistic attentions to Ophelia.

3. He chooses to accept Horatio as his best friend and he rejects all others. He treats Ophelia as though she were an indecent woman, and becomes thoroughly fed up with Rosencrantz, Guildenstern, and Polonius.

4. He undergoes various changes of mood from complete seriousness at the beginning with the players and Horatio to growing hysterical high spirits throughout the play. Finally,

he reaches a murderous seriousness as he leaves for his mother's chamber.

ACT III: SCENE 3

The King talks to Rosencrantz and Guildenstern about the danger which Hamlet's madness poses to him. Claudius plans to send them with Hamlet to England. Guildenstern says that the danger of regicide represents a "most holy and religious fear" to the very many people who depend upon the King, who "live and feed upon your majesty." Rosencrantz continues that a king is more obligated to protect himself than a private person since the welfare of many lives depend upon him. He compares the death of a king to a whirlpool which draws "what's near it with it," then to a huge wheel fixed on the summit of the highest mountain "to whose huge spokes ten thousand lesser things" are joined which attend "the boist'rous ruin" when it falls. He concludes: "Never alone/Did the king sigh, but with a general groan." The King tells them to hasten their preparations for the journey which will imprison the cause of "this fear." They leave.

COMMENT

The courtiers' remarks reflect the general Renaissance belief in "the Divine Right of Kings," which James I presented as a formal decree. This doctrine holds that kings are divinely established to ensure the welfare of their subjects and that regicide, the murder of a king, is therefore not only a political crime but a religious sin. Claudius again makes use of this doctrine in Act IV: Scene 5, as we shall see, when he says that divinity protects a king from treasonous acts. This doctrine places Hamlet's proposed revenge in a still more serious light, not merely as the sin of murder but also of regicide. Though it is true that Claudius himself committed regicide, he is now the anointed king and the horror of regicide, which an Elizabethan audience would have felt most keenly, attends him as much as it formerly did Hamlet, Sr.

Polonius enters to tell Claudius that Hamlet is going to his mother's room. Polonius is going to hide himself in Gertrude's room to spy on their conversation.

Left alone, Claudius gives way to the guilt which is tormenting him despite all his efforts to protect himself. We saw it earlier in his reaction to a chance remark by Polonius about hypocrisy. We saw it again in his reaction to the play. Now he cries out: "O, my offense is rank, it smells to heaven;/It hath the primal eldest curse upon't,/A brother's murder." The curse of Cain, who killed his brother Abel in the first biblical murder, was alienation from God. This is now Claudius' condition. He says: "Pray can I not,/Though inclination be as sharp as will./My stronger guilt defeats my strong intent."

He asks himself what the purpose of divine mercy is if not to forgive the guilty. Feeling more hopeful, he asks himself what form of prayer he can use. He realizes that he cannot simply ask God to "forgive me my foul murder," since he still possesses the results "for which I did the murder,/My crown, mine own ambition, and my queen." Though it may be possible in this "corrupted" world to be pardoned while still retaining the fruits of crime, he is fully aware that " 'tis not so above./There is no shuffling; there the action lies/In his true nature." Aware that he cannot be divinely pardoned and so be relieved of his guilt while he still enjoys the fulfillment of his royal ambition and the possession of his beloved Queen, he realizes that his only remaining possibility of pardon is to "try what repentance can," though such repentance would involve his giving up of the worldly happiness he has derived from his crown and Queen. He knows that such repentance could affect his pardon, yet is still in despair because he is too much in love with his crown and Queen to give them up: "Yet what can it when one cannot repent?/O wretched state! O bosom black as death!/O limèd soul, that struggling to be free/Art more engaged!"

His guilt is so great that he finally does pray to receive the grace which would enable him to give up the beloved effects of his crime and achieve true repentance: "Help, angels! Make assay./Bow, stubborn knees, and, heart with strings of steel,/ Be soft as sinews of the new-born babe./All may be well." He kneels in such deep prayer that he does not hear Hamlet's entrance.

When we last saw Hamlet, he was in a murderous rage against his mother. On his way to his mother's room, he accidentally comes upon Claudius alone and in prayer. He realizes that this is a perfect opportunity to perform the revenge, especially as his conscience is now clear as to Claudius' guilt (based on Claudius' reaction to the play) and he knows that he must leave immediately for England. If he does not perform the revenge now, he may never again have as good an opportunity. Seeing his opportunity, Hamlet says: "Now might I do it pat, now 'a is a-praying,/And now I'll do't." His use of the word "might" already shows his lack of inclination to kill Claudius, so he finds an immediate excuse to delay his revenge: "And so 'a goes to heaven,/And so am I revenged. That would be scanned." It is not religious scruples which prevent him from killing a man in the pious act of prayer, but the thought that, as Claudius is purging his soul, he would go to heaven upon death whereas his father's soul was unprepared for death and so went to purgatory. Unsatisfied simply to perform earthly justice, Hamlet wants his revenge to have eternal effects: he wants to ensure Claudius' damnation as well as death. It is with this thought that he puts away his drawn sword:

> Up, sword, and know thou a more horrid hent [occasion]./When he is drunk asleep, or in his rage,/Or in th' incestuous pleasure of his bed,/At game a-swearing, or about some act/That has no relish of salvation in't—/ Then trip him, that his heels may kick at heaven,/And that his soul may be as damned and black/As hell, whereto it goes.

Looking forward to this more horrid occasion, he leaves the room. Claudius rises to reveal that his prayer has not been effective, that he has not been truly able to repent: "My words fly up, my thoughts remain below./Words without thoughts never to heaven go."

COMMENT

The ethical stature of the two leading characters has been reversed. As Claudius kneels in desperate prayer for the religious strength to give up his crown and Queen, there is little doubt that at that moment he is ethically superior to the dark figure standing above him with drawn sword whose only reason for not committing murder is that such murder would not be horrible enough to satisfy his vengeance. Hamlet's vengeance here goes beyond the requirements of even the honor code, which is only concerned with the overcoming of earthly sin through the execution of earthly justice. Nowhere else is Hamlet so fully infected by the power of hell which "breathes out contagion to this world." But as this power is fully directed at this moment against his mother, it simply provides a devilish excuse to end this unforeseen delay to its true purposes.

Hamlet is placing himself at a fatal disadvantage with regards to Claudius. Hamlet's mad behavior and intrigues have led him to this moment of necessary action. His misuse of this moment allows Claudius' plan to send him away from Elsinore to take effect. No further opportunity will arise for Hamlet to take revenge without also losing his own life.

The final irony of the scene is that even Hamlet's expressed reason for the delay, the effectiveness of Claudius' prayer, proves to be invalid. Hamlet could have achieved his evil wish to send Claudius' soul to hell. From the religious perspective of Hamlet's own soul, it is well that he did not perform his revenge at this time.

Even though he might have survived the murder, his spiritual state at the time would have damned his own soul to hell.

ACT III: SCENE 4

This scene is set in Gertrude's room in the castle. Polonius, alone with Gertrude, tells her that Hamlet will be there immediately and that she should be very forceful with him. She should tell him that she has protected him as much as she could but that his behavior has been too unrestrained to be endured any longer. Polonius hides behind a hanging tapestry as Hamlet approaches.

Hamlet enters and immediately asks his mother, "What's the matter?" She answers: "Hamlet, thou hast thy father much offended." Offended by this reference to Claudius as his father, he sharply returns: "Mother, you have my father much offended." The conversation quickly proceeds with Gertrude objecting to Hamlet's "idle tongue" and Hamlet objecting to her "wicked tongue," until she finally asks, "Have you forgot me?" Though she is asking Hamlet whether he has forgotten the respect due to a mother, he answers with a bitter identification: "You are the queen, your husband's brother's wife,/ And (would it were not so) you are my mother."

Seeing that she will not get anywhere with him, she proposes to end their meeting, but Hamlet is not going to let this longed for opportunity to speak his mind to his mother get away from him so easily. Angrily forcing her to sit down, he looks so murderous that she cries out in terror for help: "What wilt thou do? Thou wilt not murder me? Help, ho!" Polonius, startled, also begins to cry for help. Hamlet, quickly drawing his sword, drives it through the tapestry, killing Polonius with the words: "How now? a rat? Dead for a ducat, dead!" The Queen cries out to ask him what he has done and Hamlet replies, "Nay, I know not. Is it the King?"

COMMENT

In the next scene, Gertrude describes what happened in the following words, which are best discussed here: "Mad as the sea and wind when both contend/Which is the mightier. In his lawless fit,/Behind the arras [tapestry] hearing something stir,/Whips out his rapier, cries, 'A rat, a rat!'/And in this brainish apprehension kills/The unseen good old man." There is little doubt that this is a good description of what actually happened. Hamlet, as he says, did not "know" what he was doing because he was temporarily insane.

Hamlet's murderous impulse toward his mother so over-powered his reason that he was on the point of murdering her when another sound distracted his attention from her long enough for his will to reassert itself and deflect the intended blow from his mother onto the nearest object. His temporary insanity at this moment is clearly shown by his incoherent cry which accompanies the murder: "How now? a rat? Dead for a ducat, dead." He does not know what he is doing, only that he must not murder his mother. It is only after the deed is done that he associates the intruding "rat" with Claudius and hopes that he may have actually accomplished his long delayed revenge without having planned it.

Hamlet is still more concerned about attacking his mother than caring about what he has done, and he immediately replies with his worst accusation against her: "A bloody deed—almost as bad, good mother,/As kill a king, and marry with his brother." The Queen is innocently shocked and confused by the meaning of such a suggestion—"As kill a King?"—and so Hamlet, simply repeating "Ay, lady, it was my word," drops the subject. He then lifts the tapestry and, seeing it is Polonius, reacts only with a casual coldness which becomes a bit mocking: "Thou wretched, rash, intruding fool, farewell!/I took thee for thy better. Take thy fortune./Thou find'st to be too busy is some danger." Immediately dismissing the whole subject, he returns to his primary object of attacking his mother with verbal daggers and says to her: "Leave wringing of your hands. Peace, sit you down/And let me wring your heart."

When the Queen asks what she can have done to deserve such rudeness from him, Hamlet begins to describe in fierce terms the immodesty, hypocrisy, and irreligiousness with which she has debased her "marriage vows." He tells her to compare the pictures of her two husbands and asks: "Have you eyes?/ Could you on this fair mountain leave to feed,/And batten on this moor?" Not only was his father far superior to Claudius but she cannot even excuse her change as resulting from love since she is too old, he claims, to be capable of such romantic feelings. Her behavior is so lacking in sense that it must be the work of a "devil" who has so blinded her that she has lost all sense of shame.

As he continues to cry out against her lack of shame, she finally begs him to "speak no more" for he is turning her eyes inward to look upon the guilt in her soul which she cannot erase. The admission of her guilt only inspires Hamlet to make his most revolting description of her act: "Nay, but to live/In the rank sweat of an enseamèd [greasy] bed,/Stewed in corruption, honeying and making love/Over the nasty sty—" Once more she interrupts him to beg him to stop tormenting her with "these words like daggers." But he continues until he forces a third anguished cry, "No more."

At this point the Ghost reappears, stopping Hamlet's relentless attack on his mother. Calling for angelic protection, he asks the "gracious figure" of the Ghost if he has come to "chide" his "tardy son" for having let his "dread command" become "lapsed in time and passion." The Ghost agrees that this is why he has had to return: "This visitation/Is but to whet thy almost blunted purpose." As Gertrude looks upon Hamlet's conversation with "amazement," having already said, "Alas, he's mad," the Ghost tells Hamlet to "speak to her." To Hamlet's question as to how she feels, she responds with concern for him since he seems to be talking to nothing. Hamlet points to the Ghost and describes its pitiful expression but she can neither see nor hear anything unusual. At this point the Ghost "steals away" out of the door and, as Hamlet continues to describe the Ghost's last motions, Gertrude concludes that what he has seen must have been a hallucination produced by his own brain, such hallucinations being a special effect of madness. Hamlet denies that he is mad and, as proof, says that he can repeat everything he has said. Then, fearing he is to lose the whole effect of his earlier tirade, he tells her that she should not flatter her soul that it is his madness which has magnified her sins for this will only increase her corruption.

COMMENT

The Ghost's reappearance here puzzles most critics. Is this the same Ghost as before or is Gertrude right that it is a hallucination? If this is a hallucination, does this cast doubt on the earlier Ghost as perhaps a product of group hysteria? If this is an objective Ghost and the same one as earlier, what is the meaning of Gertrude's inability to see it? Does her innocence protect her from seeing a diabolic agent, or has her guilt alienated her from the sight of her abused husband's Ghost? Although Hamlet speaks sanely enough after the Ghost's exit, he was becoming quite agitated again before the Ghost's entrance. Does the Ghost reappear at this point to prevent Hamlet from killing Gertrude? Does this prove that the Ghost is the genuine spirit of Hamlet, Sr., that he returns out of love for his wife, tries to shield her from any disturbance, and leaves brokenhearted at her failure to perceive him? Or is the Ghost simply a figment produced by Hamlet's own growing guilt over his preoccupation with his mother's sins which has caused his "passion" for revenge to lapse even at the most opportune moment? Shakespeare does not provide us with sufficient means for answering all of these questions. The effect of the Ghost's appearance, however, is clear. It calms Hamlet and makes Hamlet consciously aware of his misdirected efforts. The Ghost had earlier told Hamlet that he should "leave her [Gertrude] to heaven" rather than attempt to punish her. Now Hamlet does return to this more proper attitude.

Attempting to turn his mother's spirit back to her former purity, he advises her to do what Claudius had earlier himself attempted: "Confess yourself to heaven,/Repent what's past, avoid what is to come,/And do not spread the compost on the weeds/To make them ranker." Calmer now and feeling sorry for his former rudeness to her, Hamlet asks Gertrude to "forgive me this my virtue." But then, excusing himself by the needs of a corrupt time, he again shows a touch of self-righteous disrespect when he concludes that "Virtue itself of vice must pardon beg,/Yea, curb and woo for leave to do him good."

But Hamlet has achieved his wish; he has caused his mother to contritely admit her guilt to him as she now does by saying, "O Hamlet, thou hast cleft my heart in twain." Happy with his success, he tells her to "throw away the worser part of it" by never again going to his uncle's bed. By way of farewell, he says: "Once more, good night,/And when you are desirous to be blest,/I'll blessing beg of you."

COMMENT

For months Hamlet has felt himself wronged by his mother's remarriage. Now that Hamlet has returned the injury to her, he is able to achieve an emotional reconciliation with her. As she begs him for forgiveness, he can do the same to her and they can both kneel down for blessing to each other.

In this moment of harmonious reconciliation with his mother, Hamlet achieves a sense of general well-being and harmony with the universe which enables him to view his murder of Polonius in a new light. Noticing the dead body of Polonius for the first time since the murder, he says: "For this same lord,/I do repent; but heaven hath pleased it so,/To punish me with this, and this with me,/That I must be their scourge and minister."

COMMENT

This is the first time that Hamlet has expressed his harmony with heaven's purposes. Earlier he believed his desires for suicide and revenge to be opposed by heaven. Now he accepts the murder of Polonius and its consequences as being the will of heaven. He sees himself in a new role as heaven's "scourge and minister." Although he had accepted his role of revenger from the first as a means of achieving the reformation of his society, the murder it involved had seemed religiously forbidden and had involved him in a conflict between the honor code and religious commandments. Now the two seem to have become joined for him.

Polonius' murder marks the turning point in the play, both in terms of Hamlet's external situation and of his spiritual orientation: this act places him in the power of Claudius but it also gives him his sense of ordination as heaven's "scourge and minister."

Hamlet excuses the fatal effects of his new role by saying, "I must be cruel only to be kind." He says that he will take the body from the room and "will answer well the death I gave him." Aware that "worse remains behind" for him as a result of this killing, he prepares to say goodnight again but then remembers to tell his mother that she should not "let the bloat king" for "a pair of reechy kisses" cause her to confess that Hamlet is not truly mad "but mad in craft." Gertrude promises this and then Hamlet reminds her that he must leave for England. He confides in her that he neither trusts the sealed letters Claudius is sending nor his "two schoolfellows," Rosencrantz and Guildenstern, whom Claudius is also sending along with him: "They bear the mandate; they must sweep my way/And marshall me to knavery." With his new sense of divine mission, however, Hamlet is not worried for his own safety and success:

> Let it work./For 'tis the sport to have the enginer hoist with his own petar [mine], and 't shall go hard/But I will delve one yard below their mines/And blow them at the moon. O, 'tis most sweet/When in one line two crafts directly meet.

Hamlet is elated that he will somehow turn against his former friends the evil that they are now helping Claudius to work against himself. He feels no sympathy for any of Claudius' accomplices. Seeing Polonius only as a means of getting himself shipped off to England, he says most crudely: "This man shall set me packing./I'll lug the guts into the neighbor room." Then, calling Polonius "a foolish prating knave" and saying a final goodnight to his mother, he leaves the room tugging Polonius' body after him.

SUMMARY

This scene is the turning point in the play for the following reasons:
1. After having missed his opportunity to murder Claudius, Hamlet's "rash and bloody" accidental killing of Polonius makes it impossible for either Hamlet or his mother to delay Claudius' purpose to send him away to England. This makes his own task of revenge more difficult.
2. Hamlet has not only made his revenge more difficult but placed his life in danger.
3. The accidental killing of Polonius works a drastic change in Hamlet's nature. This violent act, the result of two months of mounting tension, marks the end of his downward spiritual progress and the beginning of a more positive spiritual movement. If the first appearance of the Ghost caused a hellish

state of spiritual alienation from God which reached its most extreme form in Hamlet's diabolic reasons for not killing Claudius and his equally thoughtless killing of Polonius minutes later, the appearance of the "gracious figure" of the Ghost in this scene begins to effect his reconciliation to divine purposes.

HAMLET
ACT IV

ACT IV: SCENES 1, 2, 3

The King, Queen, Rosencrantz, and Guildenstern enter another room of the castle soon after Polonius' murder. Claudius asks Gertrude why she is sighing so heavily. After asking Rosencrantz and Guildenstern to leave them alone a while, she answers with a description of Hamlet's "mad" killing of Polonius.

After a brief statement of sorrow, "O heavy deed!," Claudius immediately sees the danger Hamlet's action poses to him:

> It had been so with us, had we been there./His liberty is full of threats to all,/To you yourself, to us, to every-one./Alas, how shall this bloody deed be answered?/It will be laid to us.

Not only might Hamlet have killed either himself or Gertrude in place of Polonius, but he might yet do so if he is not immediately restrained. Claudius is afraid that he will be blamed for the murder and rightly so, for it was his "love" which prevented him from truly recognizing the danger earlier. Gertrude tells Claudius that Hamlet has gone to draw away the body and, now sorry for his deed, "weeps for what is done." Claudius tells Gertrude that he must ship Hamlet away by dawn. He calls back Rosencrantz and Guildenstern, tells them of Hamlet's action, and asks them to find Hamlet and bring him and Polonius' body into the chapel. After they leave, he tells Gertrude that they must also go and tell the council what has happened and what he means to do with Hamlet to offset any possible rumors that may arise. Very disturbed by this situation, he says as they leave, "My soul is full of discord and dismay."

Rosencrantz and Guildenstern come upon Hamlet just after he has hidden Polonius' body. Hamlet's attitude throughout the next two scenes is viciously satirical, though his satire is primarily a reaction to his renewed awareness of death through contact with Polonius' body. To their question as to what he has done with the body, Hamlet replies that he has "compounded it with dust." As they insist upon knowing, Hamlet objects to being "demanded of a sponge," and he explains this reference by saying:

> Ay, sir, that soaks up the king's countenance, his rewards, his authorities. But such officers do the king best service in the end. He keeps them, like an ape, in the corner of his jaw, first mouthed, to be last swallowed. When he needs what you have gleaned, it is but squeezing you and, sponge, you shall be dry again.

Hamlet satirically tells them that they have lost all human identity by selling their services to the King. The only reward they may expect is to be destroyed by the King who uses them, but they claim not to understand him. After continuing his contemptuous satire against both them and the body for a bit longer, he demands to be brought to the King and they all leave to go to Claudius.

The third scene begins with Claudius' explanations to some of his advisers. He tells them that he has sent for Hamlet since it is dangerous to let Hamlet continue to go about "loose" but that he must not "put the strong law on him" and "he's loved of the distracted multitude." All he can do, therefore, is to send Hamlet immediately away while giving the impression that this has been done with much deliberation. Rosencrantz enters to say that they have been unable to find where Hamlet has put the body but that they have brought Hamlet to the King. Claudius asks Hamlet where he has hidden Polonius' body. Hamlet satirically answers that Polonius is "at supper." When questioned, he explains that this supper is:

Not where he eats, but where 'a is eaten. A certain con-
vocation of politic worms are e'en at him. Your worm is
your only emperor for diet. We fat all creatures else to
fat us, and we fat ourselves for maggots. Your fat king
and your lean beggar is but variable service—two dishes,
but to one table. That's the end.

COMMENT

In Act III: Scene 3, Guildenstern had described the courtiers' dependence upon the King by using the image of
eating; he had said that they "feed upon your majesty."
In Act IV: Scene 2, Hamlet had said to Rosencrantz and
Guildenstern that the King keeps courtiers like themselves "in the corner of his jaw, first mouthed, to be last
swallowed." Such images conjure up a vision of a jungle
in which the animals are engaged in eating each other.

Other "appetites" such as sensual lust are also described
here. Hamlet had asked his mother in Act III: Scene 4,
"Could you on this fair mountain leave to feed,/And
batten on this moor?" And in Act IV: Scene 1, Claudius
had compared his "love," which kept him from impris-
oning Hamlet, to a "foul disease" which he allowed to
"feed/Even on the pith of life." Love, then, is a diseased
appetite which feeds either on oneself or on another.
Hamlet gives the ironic conclusion to this picture of
humanity as the prey to animal appetites when he says
that the result of all this feeding is simply to fatten ourselves for worms. Nothing can protect us from the final
appetite of death. This echoes the mood of Hamlet's
first soliloquy, in which he said: "How weary, stale, flat,
and unprofitable/Seem to me all the uses of this world!/
Fie on't, ah, fie, 'tis an unweeded garden/That grows to
seed. Things rank and gross in nature/Possess it merely."
The world is composed of "rank and gross" animals feeding upon one another for the "unprofitable" end of feeding worms.

Hamlet continues to discuss the conversion of men to worms to fish to men again until Claudius finally demands of him "Where is Polonius?" To this Hamlet flippantly answers: "In heaven. Send thither to see. If your messenger find him not there, seek him i' th' other place yourself. But if indeed you find him not within this month, you shall nose him as you go up the stairs into the lobby."

After sending attendants to find Polonius' body, Claudius informs Hamlet that "for thine especial safety," he is to leave immediately for England. To this Hamlet says, "Good," and Claudius adds, "So is it, if thou knew'st our purposes." Hamlet does see through Claudius' false mask of goodwill, however, as he indicates by his ambiguous reply, "I see a cherub that sees them." Feeling heaven to be on his side, he is not overly worried, and, after another bit of verbal quibbling, he leaves to prepare himself for England.

Left alone, Claudius reveals that his letter to the King of England demands "the present death of Hamlet." This alone can cure the feverish anxiety which Hamlet's free raging produces in him and which prevents him from enjoying his fortune.

COMMENT

We are not told whether Claudius' original purpose in sending Hamlet to England was to have him killed or whether this is a new purpose resulted from Hamlet's murder of Polonius. The evidence of the play would seem to argue, however, that Claudius wrote a new letter after he learned of Polonius' murder. Had he already planned this in his earlier letter to England, there should have been some mention of this when Claudius was unburdening his guilt to heaven.

Once Hamlet has killed, however, it is clear to Claudius that he can no longer allow his squeamish conscience to further endanger himself. Further, Hamlet's behavior to him is so tormenting that, after having allowed him complete liberty for four months to say or do anything while himself exercising complete self-restraint in Hamlet's presence, Claudius can no longer endure Hamlet's taunting existence. Hamlet has done everything to antagonize Claudius and break his composure. He has been more concerned about making Claudius squirm than murdering him.

While Hamlet has been throwing Claudius' soul into "discord and dismay" with his final murderous decision, Hamlet has shown no repentance. Instead, he continues to cavort in a most unseemly fashion, making a gruesome game out of hiding the body. Hamlet is in the same hysterical state as he was at the close of the play within the play and little changed from the way he was at the first. His psychological distress has thus far only resulted in an unnecessary death and his own mortal danger.

ACT IV: SCENE 4

The scene opens the following morning on a road near the Danish border. Fortinbras enters with his army and stops to talk to his Captain. He tells the Captain to go to the Danish King with his greetings and to remind him of the permission the Danish King had earlier granted Fortinbras to transport a Norwegian army over Danish territory. The Captain agrees to do this and is left alone on stage after the departure of Fortinbras and the army. Hamlet enters with Rosencrantz, Guildenstern, and others on their way to the ship which is to bear them to England.

He questions the Captain as to the nature and purpose of the army and is told that it is a Norwegian army commanded by Fortinbras on its way to conquer a small piece of Polish land "that hath in it no profit but the name." When Hamlet suggests that the Poles then "never will defend it," he is told that "it is already garrisoned." Hamlet comments that the expenditure of "two thousand souls and twenty thousand ducats" over "the question of this straw" is the sick result of "much wealth and peace." He tells the men with him to go on a little before him and is left alone on the stage.

We now come to Hamlet's last soliloquy. The sight of this army going out to fight a worthless war for a point of honor serves to stir Hamlet's shame once more at his own dishonor in having allowed his revenge to be so long delayed: "How all occasions do inform against me/And spur my dull revenge!" he says. He asks himself, "What is a man?" if his chief value and occupation be "but to sleep and feed." In line with his recent contemptuous view of man as engaged solely in eating and being eaten, he answers himself that such a man is "a beast, no more." Referring to his earlier speech to Rosencrantz and Guildenstern about humankind's wonderful qualities, he reasons that the Creator did not give man "that capability and godlike reason" so that it would grow moldy with disuse.

Realizing that people were given their abilities to accomplish something more worthy than mere bestial feeding, he asks himself whether it was "bestial oblivion" (the forgetfulness of an unaware animal) or some cowardly "scruple" produced by "thinking too precisely on th' event" which explains his lack of taking revenge. He finally must conclude: "I do not know/ Why yet I live to say, 'This thing's to do,'/Sith I have cause, and will, and strength, and means/To do 't."

In comparison with his own shameful lack of action, he now must witness the behavior of Fortinbras, "whose spirit, with divine ambition puffed," exposes his own "mortal and unsure" existence "to all that fortune, death, and danger dare" for nothing more valuable than "an eggshell." He concludes from this that to be truly "great" one must not simply be ready to fight for a sufficient and worthy cause "But greatly to find quarrel in a straw/When honor's at the stake."

With both his reason and his natural feelings excited by his father's murder and mother's dishonor, Hamlet can "let all sleep" while, to his "shame," he sees "the imminent death of twenty thousand men" for a point of honor. Having shamed himself into renewed commitment to his revenge at a time when such a revenge is almost impossible, he concludes strongly: "O, from this time forth,/My thoughts be bloody, or be nothing worth!" With this he leaves to rejoin his companions and the scene ends.

COMMENT

Just before the start of his soliloquy, Hamlet had judged Fortinbras' action as the "imposthume," the sickness produced by "much wealth and peace." The claim of the honor code upon his spirit is still strong enough, however, to produce shame at the comparison with his own inaction. While he ostensibly convinces himself of the need to pursue honor, he is also undermining the validity of the honor code at its most vulnerable point. He shows that what makes a person of honor superior to a beast is simply his willingness to "dare" any danger, and so exposing his life to death is immaterial. Although Hamlet tries to identify the honor code here with religion, calling honor "divine ambition" and claiming that honorable action is a proper use of one's God-given talents, such an identification is highly questionable and Hamlet later drops it in favor of a more proper understanding of Divine Providence. Hamlet ends by mourning the unnecessary deaths of twenty thousand men for a point of honor. Nonetheless, he is convinced by their example to pursue his own bloody path to honor. The very means by which Hamlet renews his commitment to honor serve to undermine his purpose. This is another example of Hamlet's peculiar way of rationalizing himself into momentary self-acceptance. He will be left once more with the problem: "I do not know/Why yet I live to say, 'This thing's to do,'/Sith I have cause, and will, and strength, and means/To do 't."

ACT IV: SCENE 5

This scene returns us to the castle after about a month. (This is the first lapse in time since the end of Act I. All of Act II, Act III, and the first four scenes of Act IV took place in twenty-four hours.) The Queen enters with Horatio and another gentleman. They have been trying to persuade her to see Ophelia, but Gertrude insists, "I will not speak with her." The Gentleman says that Ophelia desires to see Gertrude and that she should be pitied. When Gertrude asks what Ophelia wants with her, the Gentleman says that Ophelia speaks in a disordered way. Horatio urges that "'Twere good she were spoken with" for she is giving malicious minds unfortunate ideas. Gertrude relents and tells them to admit Ophelia. The men leave. Alone, Gertrude admits that her "sick soul" has dreaded to confront any new misfortune because of her already agitated sense of "guilt." Her speech shows that Hamlet has sparked her conscience.

Ophelia enters. Clearly insane, she asks, "Where is the beauteous majesty of Denmark?" Though Gertrude addresses her, Ophelia does not seem to know her but starts to sing two snatches of song. The first song asks how one is to know her "true-love" from another. The answer is by his clothes, which are those of a pilgrim. The second snatch of song announces, "He is dead and gone, lady," buried under grass with a stone at his heels. Ophelia continues to sing of a burial as Claudius comes in. Observing her sorry state, Claudius concludes that her insanity was caused by thoughts of her father. Ophelia does not wish to hear this and, by way of explaining the meaning of her state, sings another song. This is a rowdy ballad about a girl's loss of virginity on St. Valentine's day: her lover opens his chamber door to "Let in the maid, that out a maid/Never departed more." She tells him, "Before you tumbled me,/You promised me to wed." He answers that he would have done so had she "not come to my bed."

Ophelia weeps at the thought of her father's death and that "they would lay him i' th' cold ground," reminds them that her "brother shall know of it," and, calling for her coach, departs saying "Good night, ladies." Claudius sends Horatio to look after her and again concludes that her insanity "springs all from her father's death."

COMMENT

Although Claudius rejects the possibility of disappointed love as a cause of Ophelia's insanity, it is clear that this contributes as much to her state as her father's death. Although there is no evidence in the play that Hamlet did seduce Ophelia, Hamlet's change from offering honorable love to her to treating her as a discarded whore has evidently convinced her that she must have given him her virginity if his rejection is to be at all understood. It is clear that she did not understand her responsibility for his change of heart, since she was simply following her father's orders. These were designed to protect her from being discarded. Hamlet's treatment of her in the "nunnery" and "play" scenes affected her more deeply than was then apparent. Since her "true-love" has betrayed her trust, she no longer knows by what means to recognize him. That she does not further connect Hamlet with the murder of her father indicates the secrecy with which Claudius has concealed this fact, as he will mention almost immediately.

On the same day as she felt herself so brutally betrayed by her lover, however, she was also faced with the death of her father, a father on whose judgment she had been totally dependent for all her actions and opinions. The effect of this double tragic loss was so overwhelming that it completely destroyed her sanity.

The comparison of her circumstances with those of Hamlet at the beginning of the play should be obvious. Both were faced with a parent's death at the same time as their trust in one in whose love they had believed was betrayed. Both faced the twin evils of human existence, hypocrisy and death, at the same time. Both characters were unsettled by this double confrontation with evil. The fact that Ophelia's reaction duplicates Hamlet's serves to universalize his experience, to give it greater validity as a tragic human experience.

But the differing extent of their reactions also serves to illuminate Hamlet's stature. Ophelia's insanity reveals Hamlet's greater heroic stature: Hamlet has faced up to a tragic reality which can destroy a lesser spirit. However unsettled it made him, he has maintained his sanity. As such, Ophelia serves as a "foil" to Hamlet. In drama, a "foil" is a minor character who illuminates a central character.

Claudius tells Gertrude that Ophelia's insanity is not their only sorrow: first Polonius was slain, then Hamlet was exiled, and finally Laertes has secretly returned from France and blames Claudius for Polonius' death. This makes Laertes particularly fearful. At this a noise is heard and a messenger enters. Claudius is so unnerved by this that he calls for his "Switzers," his hired Swiss guards. The messenger tells him that he must act to save himself since Laertes has gathered a riotous rabble and overcome the King's officers. The rabble mob, having forgotten the ancient hierarchy and customs of society, want Laertes to be king. Another noise is heard; the King cries, "The doors are broke"; and Laertes and his followers enter. They demand to see the King.

Laertes tells his followers to leave him alone but guard the door, and then he says to Claudius, "O thou vile king,/Give me my father." The Queen tries to calm Laertes but he replies:

"That drop of blood that's calm proclaims me bastard." Claudius asks Laertes the cause of his rebellion. Gertrude has tried to restrain Laertes, but Claudius tells her to let him go since "There's such divinity doth hedge a king/That treason can but peep to what it would,/Act little of his will." Laertes answers with the question, "Where is my father?" Claudius answers, "Dead," and Gertrude immediately interjects, "But not by him." Laertes says:

> How came he dead? I'll not be juggled with./To hell allegiance, vows to the blackest devil,/Conscience and grace to the profoundest pit!/I dare damnation. To this point I stand,/That both worlds I give to negligence,/Let come what comes, only I'll be revenged/Most thoroughly for my father.

COMMENT

Laertes' reaction to Polonius' death stands in marked contrast to Hamlet's reaction to his father's death. Hearing that Polonius has been murdered, Laertes has gathered a mob and stormed the palace to revenge himself upon the King and seize the kingdom. That Hamlet could easily have accomplished the same revenge is shown by Claudius' earlier statement about Hamlet, "He's loved of the distracted multitude." The fact that Laertes, without any royal pretensions, could rouse a mob to overthrow the King shows how far from justice and right this behavior is.

Laertes further compromises the validity of his revenge by the terms in which he is willing to undertake it. He throws his former allegiance away, vowing himself "to hell" and to "the blackest devil." Aware of the religious implications of such revenge, he proclaims, "I dare damnation." He is unconcerned about the question of his soul's salvation as long as he can be "revenged most thoroughly for my father."

Such an attitude places Hamlet's predicament in its clearest contrast. However tempted Hamlet may have been by the power of hell, he has never been able to commit an act which he felt might damn his soul. He is not willing to commit a revenge which would involve his conscious allegiance to hell. Laertes shows us that such direct revenge on Hamlet's part would have resulted in both a social crime and spiritual damnation and that Hamlet is the better man for having delayed his revenge.

Claudius tells Laertes that he will not hinder his revenge but asks whether Laertes means to include in his revenge "both friend and foe." When Laertes answers that he is only opposed to "his enemies" and is willing to learn the true circumstances of his father's death, Claudius says that he will prove to Laertes that he is guiltless of his father's death. At this point Ophelia reenters. Laertes is shocked to discover his sister's insanity. As Ophelia sings of her father's funeral and offers flowers to everyone present, Laertes tells her, "Hadst thou thy wits, and didst persuade revenge,/It could not move thus." Continuing to sing of her father's death as she departs, she leaves a grief-stricken Laertes whom Claudius now turns to comfort.

Claudius tells Laertes that he should choose his wisest friends to judge between them as he explains the circumstances of Polonius' death. If they still find him guilty, Claudius is willing to give Laertes his crown and life, but if they find him inno-cent he says that he will be willing to help Laertes to accom-plish his revenge against the truly guilty party. Laertes agrees to this and says that he wishes a full explanation of his father's "obscure funeral" with "no noble rite nor formal ostentation." Claudius says that he shall be satisfied and then "where th' offense is, let the great axe fall." They now all leave to attend to this inquiry.

SUMMARY

This scene accomplishes the following purposes:

1. It shows us further unfortunate effects of Hamlet's murder of Polonius—Ophelia's madness and Laertes' vowed revenge.

2. Both effects serve as foils to show Hamlet's greater virtue. By showing us how similar situations shatter Ophelia's sanity and lead Laertes into behavior both criminal and damnable, we are able see Hamlet's extraordinary grip on himself. Having shown us Hamlet's flaws with the greatest of detail, Shakespeare is now beginning his rehabilitation as a tragic hero worthy of our admiration.

ACT IV: SCENES 6 AND 7

The sixth scene takes place in another room of the castle immediately following the last. Horatio has been called to this room to meet some sailors who have asked for him. He is given a letter from Hamlet which describes Hamlet's adventures at sea as follows: after they were two days at sea, a pirate ship came alongside of his ship. Some fighting ensued during which Hamlet alone boarded the pirate ship. This shows Hamlet's bravery and refutes the idea of Hamlet as a simply intellectual man. Immediately the pirate ship got clear of the Danish ship. As a result, Hamlet became their prisoner. They have treated him well, however, and Hamlet wants to reward them for the freedom they have given him. In the letter, Hamlet tells Horatio to give the King the letter he has sent. Then Horatio should follow the sailors to meet Hamlet. Horatio follows Hamlet's instructions.

The scene shifts to another room in the castle where the King has been in conference with Laertes. Laertes must now acquit Claudius since he understands "That he which hath your noble father slain/Pursued my life." Laertes grants him the appearance but asks him why he did not proceed to take justice against the offender who so threatened his own life. Claudius responds that it was "for two special reasons" which might not seem as strong to Laertes as they do to him. The first reason he states as follows:

The queen his mother/Lives almost by his looks, and for myself—/My virtue or my plague, be it either which—/She is so conjunctive to my life and soul/That, as the star moves not but in his sphere,/I could not but by her.

COMMENT

Here Claudius seems to be making a genuine confession of love for Gertrude. She is so necessary to his "life and soul" that even if his love for her destroys both his present life and eternal hope, these would both be meaningless without her. He simply cannot live without her. Such a confession may even explain the dreadful murder of his brother. His need to wholly possess his mistress may have become so great that he could no longer live without making her his wife. Such a desperate love, leading as it does to murder, may not be sanctified, but it is certainly more than the simple lust for which Hamlet and his father's Ghost condemn it. That it is love rather than lust is further shown by Claudius' tender concern to protect Gertrude from any unpleasantness.

In Gertrude's unwillingness to see the disturbed Ophelia, we may see her unwillingness to be disturbed by anything unpleasant. We can easily imagine, then, how much the unpleasant necessities of maintaining a secret adultery must have upset her. Certainly he took great pains to conceal the deed from her so that she was able to enter the marriage without too much moral difficulty. It was certainly for her sake that he tried to develop good relations with her son and even now, when her son has clearly indicated his murderous intentions against him, he cannot bear to alienate her affections by openly condemning her son to death.

The fact that all his plans for disposing of his vowed enemy must be done behind her back certainly handicaps him in dealing effectively with Hamlet. Hamlet's death, even if not ascribed to Claudius, would upset Gertrude. This might be the reason that Claudius hesitates taking these steps.

Claudius tells Laertes that the second reason he did not prosecute Hamlet was that he was afraid the "great love" the common people bear for Hamlet would cause his plans to backfire against himself "and not where I had aimed them." Laertes complains that this does not satisfy his need to revenge his father's death and sister's mental breakdown, but Claudius calms him with the assurance that he will help him accomplish his purposes.

A messenger arrives with the letters from Hamlet. Claudius is shocked but he reads the following letter to Laertes: "High and mighty, you shall know I am set naked on your kingdom. To-morrow shall I beg leave to see your kingly eyes; when I shall (first asking your pardon thereunto) recount the occasion of my sudden and more strange return. Hamlet."

COMMENT

Since Hamlet is aware of Claudius' plan to have him murdered in England, it is surprising that he should continue to act with so little concern for his own safety. Hamlet warns Claudius of his "naked," that is unarmed and unaccompanied, return into Claudius' power, thus providing Claudius with a new means to plan his destruction. What is more, Hamlet indicates his continuing hatred of Claudius by addressing him rudely as "High and mighty." Hamlet's behavior is in marked contrast to Laertes' mode of reentry into Denmark, but if it is lacking in treason it is also lacking in even the slightest degree of self-protection. Though this may seem foolish, it is the result of a new understanding he has gained while on the ship.

While both Laertes and Claudius are confused by this turn of events, they are quick to see advantage for themselves in it. Laertes says, "it warms the very sickness in my heart" that he will be able to return his injury to Hamlet. Claudius immediately conceives a new plan to dispose of Hamlet. Laertes says that he will only be fully satisfied with the plan if he might be its instrument, and Claudius replies that this is in line with his thoughts.

Before explaining his idea, Claudius asks Laertes how much he loved his father and then, very much like the Player King, reminds him that the passage of time can weaken any purpose and that one should quickly accomplish his will. To his final question as to what he would do to prove himself his father's true son, Laertes replies that he would "cut his throat i' th' church!" And Claudius agrees: "No place indeed should murder sanctuarize;/Revenge should have no bounds." Here we see most clearly the damnable nature of revenge in its essential opposition with religion. It is ironic that Claudius seconds Laertes' willingness to do that which Hamlet refrained from doing, that is killing a man in prayer, though it is also to Hamlet's discredit that his reason for not then killing Claudius was not Hamlet's reverence for piety.

Laertes' statement underscores his eagerness to "dare damnation" to effect his revenge, and in this he is in marked contrast to Hamlet. Claudius explains that his plan is to propose a fencing match between Hamlet and Laertes. Since, as just markedly shown by his letter, Hamlet is "remiss,/Most generous, and free from all contriving," he will not examine the foils and Laertes should easily be able to choose a sharply pointed rather than practice foil with which, during the course of the match, he can kill Hamlet. Laertes agrees and, not to be outdone in villainy, adds that he will also dip the tip of his foil in poison so that a mere scratch will prove fatal. Claudius suggests that if even this should fail there had better be a reserve plan so that their failure would not be apparent. He wants to prepare a poisoned cup of wine for Hamlet to drink when he becomes thirsty during the match so that "if he by chance escape your venomed stuck,/Our purpose may hold there."

COMMENT

There is surely something wrong with such a plan, for any death by a sword wound in a practice match in which the foils are supposed to have dull rounded tips could hardly be considered accidental. What is more, if Hamlet were to die after publicly drinking a drink offered by Claudius, this would also cast suspicion on Claudius. Since this plan is so inferior to the "perfect crime" of his first murder, it can only be taken as an indication of Claudius' increasing hysteria in the face of Hamlet's continued dangerous and mocking existence. Laertes is willing to go along with this plan since he feels that any kind of murder would serve to clean the stain off his "honor."

Gertrude enters with the sorrowful news that Ophelia has drowned. Ophelia had attempted to hang a wreath of wild flowers on the bough of a willow tree which had grown over a brook. The bough on which she was climbing broke, throwing her into the water below. There she lay for a time, bouyed up by her clothes while she sang snatches of old songs. At last her drenched garments pulled her down to death.

COMMENT

It might be noted that anyone who could have observed this scene well enough to have reported it to Gertrude would have been criminally negligent in not saving Ophelia from death. Though this problem can be argued away by considering Gertrude's tale as a stage convention for reporting an event which could not be presented on stage, the fact remains that it is rumored that Ophelia's death was the result of suicide. This is reflected in the truncated form of her funeral. We are then left with the possibility that Gertrude was told a story which would not upset her, or that she herself elaborated a story which placed Ophelia's death in its least unpleasant light, whether for her own benefit or for Laertes'. These possibilities are in line with what we know of Gertrude's character. Whether consciously or not, Ophelia's mental condition resulted in her death. This again serves as a foil to Hamlet's rejection of the temptation to commit suicide.

Laertes tries to restrain his tears at hearing of his sister's death but finally is forced to quickly leave the room. Claudius and Gertrude quickly follow to try to comfort him.

SUMMARY

These last two scenes serve to sharply distinguish Hamlet from Claudius and Laertes. While Hamlet is, as Claudius notes, "Most generous, and free from all contriving," Claudius and Laertes busy themselves with treacherously planning his death. The rehabilitation of Hamlet begun in the previous scene is continued in these scenes, even in the face of Ophelia's death.

HAMLET
ACT V

ACT V: SCENE 1

The scene takes place in a graveyard near the castle at Elsinore on the following day. Two clownish gravediggers are discussing the funeral rites of the lady for whom they are preparing a grave. It appears that she is to have a Christian burial, although they think she committed suicide. They resent the preferential treatment she is getting:

> And the more pity that great folk should have count'nance in this world to drown or hang themselves more than their even-Christen. Come, my spade. There is no ancient gentlemen but gard'ners, ditchers, and grave-makers. They hold up Adam's profession.

The chief gravedigger sends the other for some liquor. He continues to dig while singing a song of youthful love: "In youth when I did love, did love,/Methought it was very sweet." Hamlet and Horatio enter. Hamlet is surprised that the gravedigger is so lacking in "feeling of his business, that 'a sings at grave-making." Horatio explains this as a product of "custom" and Hamlet agrees.

The gravedigger throws up a skull and Hamlet reflects on the vanity of human wishes:

> How the knave jowls it to the ground, as if 'twere Cain's jawbone, that did the first murder! This might be the pate of a politician, which this ass now o'erreaches; one that would circumvent God, might it not? . . . Or of a courtier, which could say "Good morrow, sweet lord!"

Here, Hamlet seems to be thinking of Claudius and such courtiers as Polonius, Rosencrantz, and Guildenstern. Claudius has tried to "circumvent God" through a brother's murder and yet all he shall finally gain is a death like that which Hamlet has already awarded to Claudius' courtiers, as we shall soon see. Hamlet's readiness to identify the skull he sees being rudely thrown about with Claudius' shows us that Hamlet has Claudius' coming death very firmly in mind.

As Hamlet continues to reflect on the generality of death, however, he becomes upset by it: "Did these bones cost no more the breeding but to play at loggets with 'em? Mine ache to think on't." He finally asks the gravedigger whose grave it is. When the gravedigger answers that though "I do not lie in't, yet it is mine," Hamlet replies in as humorous a vein, "Thou dost lie in't, to be in't and say it is thine. 'Tis for the dead, not for the quick; therefore thou liest." Here we see Hamlet once more moving quickly from melancholy to punning wit, but his mood is more controlled, his melancholy brief, his wit more playful. Hamlet seems to have himself in better control.

After finally being told that the grave is being prepared for a woman, Hamlet asks the gravedigger how long he has been in his job. The gravedigger replies that it has been thirty years, that he began on "that day that our last king Hamlet overcame Fortinbras," which was also "the very day that young Hamlet was born." Here we have our first indication of Hamlet's exact age. As Hamlet is soon to reach his tragic end, it is important to establish his significance as a grown man rather than a youth. Then we know that his actions are motivated by mature consideration rather than youthful disillusionment.

The gravedigger comes upon the skull of someone he knew, Yorick, the king's jester, who had died twenty-three years before. Hamlet takes the skull and says to Horatio:

> Alas, poor Yorick! I knew him, Horatio, a fellow of infi-
> nite jest, of most excellent fancy. He hath borne me on
> his back a thousand times. And now how abhorred in

my imagination it is! My gorge rises at it. Here hung those lips that I have kissed I know not how oft. Where be your gibes now?

Hamlet is reminded that he has already lived a full generation. If death is waiting for Claudius, it may also be waiting for him as well. When Hamlet begins to wonder whether one's imagination can "trace the noble dust of Alexander till 'a find it stopping a bunghole," Horatio sanely advises him that "'Twere to consider too curiously, to consider so." Hamlet, however, continues to elaborate this subject, just as he had after Polonius' death, until he is interrupted by the approach of a funeral party led by the King. He notes that the "maimed rites" indicate the funeral of a suicide and he decides to withdraw with Horatio to observe the event unseen.

The King, Queen, Laertes, a Doctor of Divinity, and other lords enter with the corpse. Laertes suddenly cries out: "What ceremony else?" The Doctor of Divinity explains that since "her death was doubtful," they have enlarged her funeral rites as much as they could and are at least burying her with prayers in sanctified ground rather than throwing rocks on her unsanctified grave. Disgusted, Laertes is forced to agree to the funeral but tells the Doctor, "A minist'ring angel shall my sister be/When thou liest howling." Shocked, Hamlet says, "What, the fair Ophelia?" Gertrude scatters flowers on Ophelia's grave with the sad reflection: "I hoped thou shouldst have been my Hamlet's wife./I thought thy bride-bed to have decked, sweet maid,/And not have strewed thy grave."

Her mention of Hamlet enrages Laertes with the remembrance of Hamlet's guilt for all his family's woes, and he exclaims: "O, treble woe/Fall ten times treble on that cursèd head/Whose wicked deed thy most ingenious sense/Deprived thee of!" At the thought of her fate he longs to embrace her once more and, leaping into the grave, calls upon the gravediggers to bury him with her under such a mountain that it "o'ertop old

Pelion" or Olympus itself. (This refers to the mythical war in which the Titans attempted to pile the mountain Ossa upon the mountain Pelion in order to reach the heaven of the Olympian gods.)

Aroused, as he later says, "into a tow'ring passion" by the ostentatious display of Laertes' grief, Hamlet comes forward. Hamlet questions Laertes' right to such grief when he, "Hamlet the Dane" is there, and leaps into the grave after Laertes. Laertes begins to fight with him, saying, "The devil take thy soul!" Hamlet objects to this prayer and his reply further indicates his self-awareness of his dangerous tendency to rashness: "Thou pray'st not well./I prithee take thy fingers from my throat,/For though I am not splenitive and rash,/Yet have I in me something dangerous,/Which let thy wisdom fear." Though he has leaped belligerently into the grave, he tries to control himself from fighting with Laertes. After they have parted and left the grave, however, Hamlet says that he is willing to fight Laertes to the death on the subject of his love for Ophelia. Though Laertes holds him guilty of her death, he proclaims: "I loved Ophelia. Forty thousand brothers/Could not with all their quantity of love/Make up my sum." Hamlet is willing to match any attempt on Laertes' part to prove his love for Ophelia. If Laertes wishes "to outface me with leaping in her grave," so will he. Hamlet will call down as much earth to cover them as will "make Ossa like a wart!" He concludes his unseemingly harangue with the words "I'll rant as well as thou," at which point his mother explains to Laertes that "this is mere madness."

She says that for "a while the fit will work on him" and then, "as patient as the female dove," he will silently "sit drooping." Upon hearing his mother's words, Hamlet calms himself sufficiently to ask Laertes: "What is the reason that you use me thus?/I loved you ever." With no apparent awareness of his responsibility for the deaths of Laertes' father and sister and for his present disruption of Ophelia's funeral, he concludes:

"But it is no matter./Let Hercules himself do what he may,/ The cat will mew, and dog will have his day." Believing that no amount of heroic endeavor would keep a low animal like Laertes from making noises at him, he abruptly turns from them and leaves.

COMMENT

Although Hamlet's tender regard for Ophelia is momentarily revived at the moment he becomes aware of her death, the memory of former love immediately becomes mingled with a sense of guilt when Laertes accuses him of responsibility for her death. Though Hamlet has not been told the reasons for Ophelia's death and so might not immediately guess his responsibility for her apparent suicide, he tries to suppress the sense of guilt occasioned by Laertes' words by clutching that memory of former feeling. This way, he can prove his love superior to that anyone else can feel.

Angered by Laertes' loud show of grief—even as it stings his conscience—Hamlet tries to evade his guilt by affirming his deep love for Ophelia and the superiority of his love to Laertes' feelings for his sister. He challenges Laertes to this test of love. Aware only of his own feelings, first for Ophelia, now for Laertes, he cannot understand why Laertes should be treating him so rudely: "What is the reason that you use me thus?/I loved you ever." When Laertes refuses to condone Hamlet's present and past behavior, Hamlet's self-righteous involvement with his own feelings climaxes in the contemptuous insults he hurls at Laertes in apparent requital for his own wrongs. Hamlet is not sympathetic toward anyone whom he believes to be wronging him. As he acted this way with Polonius, Ophelia, and, as we shall soon see, Rosencrantz and Guildenstern, so does he here with Laertes.

Claudius tells Horatio to follow Hamlet and then tells Laertes to keep his patience in the memory of the previous night's conference and in the assurance that very soon "this grave shall have a living monument," that is, the life of Hamlet. Upon this note of discord between Hamlet and Laertes, the scene ends.

SUMMARY

This scene has the following important aspects:

1. The gravediggers' joking about death provides some comic relief just before the final scene of multiple deaths. It also prepares us thematically for the play's outcome.

2. In Hamlet's easy familiarity with the gravediggers, as earlier with the players and pirates and with his less well-born college friends, we see the true gentility of one who, being "to the manner born," is able to forget his special aristocratic privileges and become "even-Christen" with all men of good will. This contrasts Hamlet with Laertes, who always stands upon "ceremony."

3. When Hamlet offers to duel with Laertes and then asks him his grievance, Laertes has the opportunity to explain himself honestly to Hamlet. Laertes can then either accept their mutual love for Ophelia as reason for their reconciliation or attempt to revenge his father's death in an honorable duel to the death. Laertes, however, is so angry that he continues to nurse his secret and ignoble revenge. Claudius can easily use Hamlet's irrational behavior as a means of strengthening Laertes' allegiance to himself and insuring the speedy enactment of their plan.

ACT V: SCENE 2

The final scene takes place in a major hall of the castle at Elsinore soon after the funeral. Hamlet enters and explains his recent behavior to Horatio. He immediately comes to the important events on shipboard, which, in his letter to Horatio, he had said would make Horatio "dumb." What he did on shipboard was rash and he now explains the insights he drew from his experience:

And praised be rashness for it—let us know,/Our indiscretion sometime serves us well/When our deep plots do pall, and that should learn us/There's a divinity that shapes our ends,/Rough-hew them how we will—

Shakespeare has Horatio underscore the significance of these statements by saying, "That is most certain."

COMMENT

Hamlet has learned that people cannot carve out their own destiny—this is ultimately shaped by Providence. Such an idea is not new to him or to the play, for he had earlier expressed it in the following lines given to the Player King: "Our wills and fates do so contrary run/ That our devices still are overthrown;/Our thoughts are ours, their ends none of our own." The "devices" and "deep plots" by which people attempt to shape their fate cannot achieve final success since people must recognize that they are dependent upon Divine Providence. Hamlet's experiences now cause him to accept this idea with full conviction.

For Shakespeare, the essential moral distinction between people is not simply between those who do good and those who do evil, but between those who recognize their dependence upon the divine will and are willing to follow it and those who reject the idea of their dependence upon God and believe that they alone must bear the responsibility for shaping their destiny.

Shakespeare's villains begin their course with an attitude which sounds very sensible to modern ears, that if there is such a thing as divinity it is quite irrelevant to human actions and that if people are to achieve anything in this world they can only do so through their own efforts. But such an attitude places people alone in the universe and causes them to see themselves as its center. This cosmic loneliness joined to a necessary ego-centricity then leads to a person's alienation from the community. There is nothing, therefore, which can hinder a person from attempting to achieve his desires at whatever the cost to others. At this point a person becomes capable of any villainy. This is the genesis of Shakespeare's villains and, though less articulated by Claudius, also explains his behavior.

Next, Hamlet explains that one night on shipboard he felt so restless that he "rashly" left his cabin, found his way in the dark to the cabin of Rosencrantz and Guildenstern, discovered their package of letters, and returned to his own cabin. Once there, he was "so bold" as to "unseal/Their grand commission; where I found, Horatio—/Ah, royal knavery!—an exact command" that without any loss of time, "No, not to stay the grinding of the axe,/My head should be struck off." Surrounded as he was "with villainies," he again acted upon impulse without any prior planning of this course of action: "Or I could make a prologue to my brains,/They had begun the play." Although he had earlier considered fine penmanship the mark of a lower mind and had tried to forget his early training in fine handwriting, this training now served him well for it enabled him to write a formal state document. He immediately "devised a new commission, wrote it fair," and demanded of the English King that without any debating of this order "He should the bearers put to sudden death,/Not shriving time allowed." When Horatio asks him how he was able to seal this forged commission, Hamlet replies, "Why, even in that was heaven ordinant./I had my father's signet in my purse." Hamlet sees this as a sign of heaven's hand in these events.

Horatio notes in what must be a faintly disapproving tone, "So Guildenstern and Rosencrantz go to't." But Hamlet strongly justifies his actions with words:

Why, man, they did make love to this employment./ They are not near my conscience; their defeat/Does by their own insinuation grow./'Tis dangerous when the baser nature comes/Between the pass and fell incensèd points/Of mighty opposites.

Horatio's next comment, "Why, what a king is this!" enables Hamlet to come to the real issue on his conscience, the question of regicide:

Does it not, think thee, stand me now upon—He that hath killed my king, and whored my mother,/Popped in between th' election and my hopes,/Thrown out his angle for my proper life,/And with such coz'nage—is't not perfect conscience/To quit him with this arm? And is't not to be damned/To let this canker of our nature come/ In further evil?

COMMENT

We see from this last speech that Hamlet had not earlier been convinced of the rightness of killing a king. By waiting until this time, however, and forcing Claudius to show his hand, he now has solid ground for proceeding to enact not simply a possibly damnable personal revenge, but clear justice. The initial reason for action, Claudius' regicide against Hamlet's father, has been superceded by Claudius' attack upon his own life. Now, he is acting in self-protection to openly rid Denmark of a king who has gained his throne through murder. Not to act in this clear case of justice would now be as damnable as personal revenge on behalf of family honor might earlier have been.

But while it is commendable that Hamlet is so concerned to establish the justice of his actions against Claudius, it is all the more surprising that his planned murders of Rosencrantz and Guildenstern "are not near my conscience." Though his present attitude toward them is less offensive than was his attitude toward Polonius immediately after his murder of him, his justification is the same: "Take thy fortune./Thou find'st to be too busy is some danger." Once Rosencrantz and Guildenstern have forfeited his trust, Hamlet has no further use for them.

If it is true that they were carrying sealed orders for his murder, there is no evidence that they had any knowledge of the contents of this commission. Nor does their compliance with Claudius' wishes constitute definite proof of their baseness. The King had sent for them. Claudius had proved himself a good ruler, concerned for his people's welfare. He seemed to be showing a benevolent concern for Hamlet's health in asking them to help him to understand and thereby cure Hamlet's disorder. During their single day at court, Hamlet's wild behavior after the performance of the play, his murder of Polonius, and subsequent display of irrational playfulness could only have convinced them that Hamlet was dangerously mad and that Claudius was taking the most lenient course open to a king forced to protect himself. Though they ally themselves so fully with the King's purposes after the murder of Polonius as to appear high-handed with Hamlet, there is no other way for them to act since Hamlet has grown increasingly belligerent toward them during the course of the day.

It would seem, then, that Hamlet is being unfair in condemning Rosencrantz and Guildenstern to death for their apparently innocent obedience to their King. But Hamlet feels that his revenge should extend to all the accomplices of Claudius' illegitimate reign.

Horatio stresses the practical need of speedy action since

Claudius will undoubtedly be soon informed of the result of his mission to England. Hamlet agrees: "It will be short; the interim is mine./And a man's life's no more than to say 'one.'"

COMMENT

Hamlet feels quite confident that he will accomplish his task before the ambassador from England arrives. From Hamlet's behavior here, however, it is also clear that he has made no plan for killing Claudius. In accordance with his new understanding of the divine control over human events, Hamlet has placed his entire reliance upon Providence, confident that the "divinity that shapes our ends" will arrange the circumstances necessary for his action.

Now that his revenge seems so close to being accomplished, Hamlet suddenly becomes aware of Laertes' just grievance against himself and feels "very sorry" that "to Laertes I forgot myself." He excuses his treatment of Laertes on the grounds that "the bravery [ostentation] of his grief did put me/Into a tow'ring passion" and hopes to be able to gain Laertes' forgiveness and vows, "I'll court his favors."

The courtier Osric enters with a message of welcome from Claudius. Osric doffs his hat before Hamlet as he is about to deliver his message, but Hamlet democratically tells him to return his hat to his head. When Osric refuses on the grounds that "it is very hot," Hamlet begins to make fun of him as he earlier had with Polonius, insisting first that it is cold and then hot, Osric agreeing to everything Hamlet says. Finally Hamlet prevails on Osric to wear his hat. Ostric tries to get to the point of his coming, the "great wager" the King has placed on Hamlet's head. When he begins to extol Laertes' merits in the most ridiculously affected manner, however, Hamlet cannot restrain himself from imitating Osric's absurd manner of speech. But Osric is too foolishly vain of his own accomplishments to realize that Hamlet is making fun of him and replies: "Your

lordship speaks most infallibly of him." Hamlet continues to
mock Osric, to Horatio's delight, until he finally gets the
bewildered Osric to come to the point of the wager.

Regaining his speech with all its affectation, Osric now explains that Claudius has wagered six Barbary horses against
six French rapiers and poniards that in a fencing match between Hamlet and Laertes, of a dozen passes, Laertes would
not exceed Hamlet by three hits. The odds are laid twelve to
nine in Hamlet's favor. Osric wants to know whether Hamlet
is willing for this match to come "to immediate trial," and
Hamlet answers that he is willing to have the foils brought
immediately to this very hall and to begin the match.

After Osric leaves, Hamlet and Horatio continue to comment
on the comic absurdity of courtiers like Osric until another
lord enters from Claudius to know whether Hamlet still wishes
to play immediately with Laertes or would "take longer time."
As Hamlet says that he is ready if the King so wishes, the lord
informs him that the King, Queen, and court are coming to
the match and that the Queen desires Hamlet to greet Laertes
in a gentlemanly fashion before they start to play. Hamlet
says that he will follow this instruction and the lord leaves.

When they are once more alone, Horatio suggests that
Hamlet will "lose this wager," but Hamlet disagrees as he has
been "in continual practice" since Laertes went to France and
should be able to "win at the odds." Nonetheless, he feels a
premonition of danger in his heart, though he rejects such
"foolery." Horatio advises Hamlet to obey his intuitions and
says that he will delay the match on the grounds that Hamlet
is not well. But Hamlet replies:

> Not a whit, we defy augury. There is special providence
> in the fall of a sparrow. If it be now, 'tis not to come; if
> it be not to come, it will be now; if it be not now, yet it
> will come. The readiness is all. Since no man of aught
> he leaves knows, what is't to leave betimes? Let be.

COMMENT

This is a key speech because it is Hamlet's most complete statement of his belief in the providential nature of all events. As every event down to "the fall of a sparrow" has been determined by the special concern of Providence, one will die when it has been appointed. Moreover, no man "knows" anything of what he has left behind once he is dead. Therefore, people should not be concerned about death. The important thing is to achieve a state of "readiness."

The proof that Hamlet has achieved this "readiness" is given in the last words of this speech, "Let be." When earlier faced with the horror of death, his spirit refused to let it be. Rather than accept the evils of existence, he felt impelled to either suicide or revenge, though these impulses showed "a will most incorrect to heaven." Though this consciousness of evil warped his sensitive nature to the point that he felt "I must be cruel only to be kind" and acted as such, his spirit also began to develop a new healing consciousness of the providential nature of reality. Hamlet no longer views the "Everlasting" as a harsh, damning lawgiver whose creation became a sterile farce. Now, he sees a sanctifying Providence, inspiring people with a new liberation of spirit to do and affirm the work of the "Divinity."

The King and court arrive. While the hall is being prepared for the fencing match, Claudius places Laertes' hand into Hamlet's in an apparent bid for their reconciliation. Hamlet begins in the most cordial terms by saying: "Give my your pardon, sir. I have done you wrong,/But pardon't, as you are a gentleman." He attempts to excuse his behavior on the grounds of madness, a madness which punishes him as much as his victims. In his own defense, Hamlet says: "Let my disclaiming from a purposed evil/Free me so far in your most generous thoughts/That I have shot my arrow o'er the house/And hurt my brother."

Laertes admits that he is "satisfied in nature," but he is not willing to make a formal reconciliation with Hamlet until "some elder masters of known honor" can show him by precedents that his honor will not be stained by such a peace. Until that time, however, he says that he will "not wrong" Hamlet's offering of love. Hamlet embraces Laertes' reply and is ready to begin "this brother's wager." They call for the foils and, making a pun on the word "foil," Hamlet generously tells Laertes, "I'll be your foil," his own poor performance making Laertes' skill shine the more brightly. As they go to choose the foils, Hamlet seems to convince Laertes that he does not "mock" him. Hamlet is satisfied with the foil he chooses but Laertes is not. He chooses another foil while Claudius explains to Hamlet once more the terms of the wager. As they prepare to play, Hamlet asks whether the foils are all alike, that is, have dulled ends, and Osric replies, "Ay, my good lord."

COMMENT

In Laertes' reply to Hamlet's apology, we see again his primary concern with "ceremony" and "terms of honor" rather than with the deeper emotional reality of a situation. Though Hamlet seems to have genuinely touched Laertes and perhaps confused his purposes, it does not prevent Laertes from choosing the fatally sharp and poisoned sword while Claudius connives to distract Hamlet's attention. In his concern for the outward appearances of honor, then, Laertes is dishonoring. He goes against his sworn word not to "wrong" Hamlet's love. Osric's assurance to Hamlet about the similarity of the foils suggests that he is also in on the plot, but it is possible that Claudius or Laertes may have grouped the swords without his knowledge.

Claudius calls for wine and says that if Hamlet hits Laertes in the first three exchanges "the king shall drink to Hamlet's better breath." He will then drop a rich "union" (pearl) into the cup for Hamlet while "the kettle to the trumpet speak,/

The trumpet to the cannoneer without,/The cannons to the heavens, the heaven to earth."

Hamlet and Laertes begin to play. On the first exchange Hamlet scores, as Osric says, "A hit, a very palpable hit." The drum, trumpets, and cannon sound. The King stops the duel to drink to Hamlet, drop the pearl into the cup, and offer the ceremonial cup to him.

COMMENT

The pearl which Claudius drops in the cup after he drinks from it is apparently the means by which the drink is poisoned. We may wonder at Claudius' haste to poison Hamlet. This can only be explained by his loss of faith in Laertes' willingness or ability to fulfill his part of their agreement. Perhaps Claudius believed Laertes' promise of fair play to Hamlet; perhaps he senses in Laertes' performance a hesitance to play up to his full ability. Certainly, Laertes' fencing is so poor that, by the third exchange, even Hamlet taunts him.

Hamlet, however, refuses to join Claudius in a toast and asks that the cup be set by awhile until he finishes the next bout. He calls for the beginning of the second bout and immediately makes "another hit," as Laertes admits.

Claudius tells Gertrude "our son shall win." In apparent delight over his son's good performance, she goes to wipe Hamlet's brow with her handkerchief. She picks up the cup and tells Hamlet that she too is going to toast his fortune. To this action Hamlet exclaims, "Good madam!" but Claudius calls out to her imperiously, "Gertrude, do not drink." She insists, however, "I will, my lord; I pray you pardon me." In silent agony, Claudius reflects: "It is the poisoned cup; it is too late." Hamlet still does not wish to interrupt his fencing and says to her, "I dare not drink yet, madam—by and by." She goes to wipe his face once more before he starts to play again.

COMMENT

It has been suggested that Gertrude acts in a spirit of motherly self-sacrifice because she suspects the cup's poisoned contents and that Hamlet's exclamation reflects his own suspicions. But such suspicions would hardly account for their subsequent actions, Hamlet's insistence upon continuing his match with Laertes and Gertrude's coming forth to wipe his brow once more. It seems more likely, therefore, that Gertrude is acting with fatal consistency to her character. We have seen that Gertrude tends to withdraw from any unpleasant truth and to delude herself that all is well. She knows that Laertes means to revenge his father's murder and probably suspects that Claudius has explained Hamlet's responsibility for Polonius' death to him. Her inability to face any unpleasant truth is her tragic flaw and it now destroys her.

At this fateful moment Claudius might yet have prevented her death by confessing to the poison. Since he is unable to protect her without giving himself away, he chooses his own survival and his throne over his love. As a result, he can only look on in shocked horror at the ironic twisting of destiny which brings the poison to her lips instead of to Hamlet's as he had designed it. With all this, he too deludes himself into thinking that he can still shape his ends.

As the third round is about to start, Laertes tells Claudius that he will hit Hamlet in this bout. Claudius replies that he doubts it and Laertes admits to himself, "And yet it is almost against my conscience." Hamlet playfully taunts Laertes about his poor performance, "You but dally," to which Laertes responds, "Say you so? Come on." Playing now to his best ability, Laertes can only bring Hamlet to a draw by the end of the bout. Enraged, he lunges at Hamlet after the close of the round—"Have at you now!"—and manages to wound Hamlet. When Hamlet realizes by his wound that Laertes has been fencing with an illegally sharp sword, he returns the attack with such fury that he gains control of the poisoned weapon in exchange for his own with which he seriously wounds Laertes.

COMMENT

Laertes is destroyed by his false pride and honor. As Laertes' better instincts begin to disturb his conscience, there is a moment when he might have dropped his vindictive plan against Hamlet in the true spirit of reconciliation which he had pledged. But at this crucial moment, Hamlet makes the fatal mistake of playfully taunting Laertes. This immediately touches Laertes' sensitive pride about outward appearances. Playing now as best he can, Laertes feels so dishonored by his inability to defeat Hamlet that he completely dishonors himself by attacking Hamlet after the close of the bout. Jealousy, pride, and a false sense of honor have overridden the better promptings of his conscience. As a result, he truly dishonors himself and is fatally wounded. The price of venging himself against Hamlet, as he soon realizes, is his own destruction.

Though Hamlet is anxious to continue his fight with Laertes despite Claudius' attempts to have them parted, the fight is finally stopped by the fall of the Queen. Horatio also notes that "they bleed on both sides" and asks Hamlet how he is. Osric also asks Laertes how he is and Laertes replies: "Why, as a woodcock to mine own springe [trap], Osric./I am justly killed with mine own treachery." Hamlet, not as seriously wounded as Laertes, is more concerned about his mother, but Claudius answers his query by saying that Gertrude is only swooning at the sight of their blood. When she hears Claudius' false words, the dying Gertrude cries out: "No, no, the drink, the drink! O my dear Hamlet!/The drink, the drink! I am poisoned."

COMMENT

Claudius' lie about his wife's fatal condition clears Gertrude's mind of her own delusions. She suddenly understands that she has been poisoned by the drink her husband prepared for her son. Even more important, she realizes that to protect himself Claudius allowed her to drink poison and is now lying to cover his guilt. In her final moments she fully faces the evil that she had tried to avoid seeing in Claudius and allies herself completely with her son against Claudius.

With the Queen's full confession of Claudius' villainy before the assembled court, the enraged Hamlet attempts to assume control of the state and begin an immediate inquiry into Claudius' guilt: "O villainy! Ho! let the door be locked./Treachery! See it out." But Laertes now falls with the words, "Hamlet, thou art slain." He explains that the sword in Hamlet's hands is not only sharp but poisoned and that Hamlet has no more than "half an hour's life." Laertes is also doomed, for his "foul practice/Hath turned itself on me." For both their deaths and for the poisoning of the Queen, he cries out to all, "The king, the king's to blame." Hearing that his life is now forfeit, Hamlet turns his poisoned sword on the King with the words, "The point envenomed too?/Then, venom, to thy work." The fatally poisoned Claudius speaks his last words. "O, yet defend me, friends, I am but hurt."

COMMENT

Hamlet was about to present his own evidence against Claudius when Laertes informed him that he was poisoned. But if Hamlet was not expecting to die, how much more dreadful is Claudius' state of spiritual unpreparedness. Having just wronged his beloved wife by blatantly lying about her condition, he now descends to the more desperate lie of self-delusion, saying that he is "but hurt." Unprepared to die, Claudius desperately clings to the delusion of possible life as before he had clung to the hope of preserving his throne while helplessly watching his wife die. Trying to play god to the end, he has only succeeded in destroying both his wife and himself.

Hamlet quickly dispatches Claudius with the poisoned drink he had prepared. Forcing this down his throat, he cries: "Here, thou incestuous, murd'rous, damnèd Dane,/Drink off this potion. Is thy union here?/Follow my mother." As the King dies, Laertes says that "he is justly served" by the poison he had prepared for Hamlet. He turns to Hamlet with his last words: "Exchange forgiveness with me, noble Hamlet./Mine and my father's death come not upon thee,/Nor thine on me!" The dying Hamlet accepts the dead Laertes' wish as he says: "Heaven make thee free of it! I follow thee."

COMMENT

Hamlet had earlier referred to Laertes as "a very noble youth" and now Laertes fulfills that potential nobility which had been buried under the false honor of appearances he had learned from his father. Laertes rises to the true reconciliation which Hamlet had earlier desired but which Laertes had fatally delayed out of false pride and jealousy. Laertes is won completely to Hamlet's side. This final movement of Gertrude and Laertes to Hamlet's side serves to redeem them from the guilt of their complicity with Claudius, if not to save their lives. It also serves to rehabilitate Hamlet in our eyes. Gertrude's "dear Hamlet" and Laertes' "noble Hamlet" remain our final image of Shakespeare's transformed hero.

Hamlet wishes he could more fully explain his act to the horrified spectators but, "as this fell sergeant, Death,/Is strict in his arrest," he tells Horatio that he must "report me and my cause aright/To the unsatisfied."

COMMENT

Hamlet's "revenge" for his father's murder is no longer the motive for his action. What finally unleashes Hamlet's lethal thrust is his recognition that he has fallen a mortal victim to Claudius' plot against him: "The point envenomed too?/Then, venom to thy work." Though he had meant to take judicial action against Claudius for his responsibility in the death of his mother and the plot against his own life, he now uses the little time left him to avenge his own murder. Then Hamlet avenges his mother's death with the same drink which had poisoned her. Condemning Claudius for only those actions of which the court has objective knowledge, his incestuous marriage to his brother's widow and her murder, Hamlet's final words to Claudius are: "Follow my mother."

But if Hamlet has finally caught Claudius in an act "that has no relish of salvation in't," he transcends the earlier spirit of revenge which might also have caused his own damnation. He has not committed the premeditated revenge commanded by the Ghost. Hamlet rises to the height of true nobility by understanding and accepting the "divinity that shapes our ends." He believed that heaven would arrange events to enable him to fulfill its will and his own. Although it was at the cost of his own life and his mother's, Hamlet was able to execute Claudius in the most "perfect conscience" for these public events alone.

For once, Horatio attempts to go against Hamlet's wishes. Objecting that he is "more an antique Roman than a Dane" (that is, a Stoic who believes in suicide rather than survival with shame), Horatio attempts to emulate Hamlet's nobility by drinking the remaining poison and following his beloved friend to death. But with his last strength Hamlet forcibly wrests the poisoned cup from Horatio's hands: "Give me the cup. Let go. By heaven, I'll ha't." Death may provide final happiness, but if Horatio truly loves him he would better follow his example by continuing the painful process of living and justifying Hamlet's name: "If thou didst ever hold me in thy heart,/

Absent thee from felicity awhile,/And in this harsh world draw thy breath in pain,/To tell my story."

Hamlet hears a "warlike noise." Osric explains that it is Fortinbras' troops, returned from their conquest in Poland, greeting the ambassadors from England they met on their way to Elsinore. The poison has so overcome him, however, that Hamlet fears he will not live long enough to hear the result of his substituted commission to the English King. As his death will also mark the end of the Danish royal line, he now turns his last thoughts to the question of the Danish succession, for he is now de facto ruler of Denmark and must attend to the good of his state: "I do prophesy th' election lights/On Fortinbras. He has my dying voice." Horatio is to tell Fortinbras of this and of all that has happened because for Hamlet "the rest is silence." As Hamlet dies, Horatio bids farewell to his noble friend in the full confidence of his spiritual salvation: "Now cracks a noble heart. Good night, sweet prince,/And flights of angels sing thee to thy rest!" Right after Hamlet dies, Fortinbras enters with the ambassadors from England.

COMMENT

The fact that without any plan Hamlet was able to accomplish his purpose in the allowed time shows that, within the universe of Shakespeare's play, Hamlet's insight into the nature of reality is as valid as it is profound. The moral significance of this new understanding is given further validity by the spiritual change it has worked in Hamlet. Though Hamlet still views the world as "harsh," he now rejects any suggestion of suicide, using his last strength to insist upon the necessity for Horatio to live, however painful it may be to continue to draw breath. Hamlet's own last thoughts are his most life affirming. He is concerned for the healthy continuance of the state whose evils he has scourged with such fatal consequences for himself. Though his life was tortured by the black vision of death, he dies with the dearly earned vision of the high value of life. Though dreadfully tempted by the powers of damnation, his spirit has most nobly won its salvation.

As Fortinbras views the royal deaths he can only ask, "O proud Death,/What feast is toward in thine eternal cell." To tie up all the loose ends, the ambassador from England informs us "that Rosencrantz and Guildenstern are dead." Horatio now suggests that the bodies be arranged in state and placed on view after which he can tell them "Of carnal, bloody, and unnatural acts,/Of accidental judgments, casual slaughters,/Of deaths put on by cunning and forced cause,/And, in this upshot, purposes mistook/Fall'n on th' inventors' heads."

Fortinbras is anxious to hear of this but also takes the opportunity to state his claim to the throne of Denmark. Horatio says that he has cause to speak of this as well but that first the funeral arrangement should be made to quiet "men's minds." Fortinbras orders four captains to "bear Hamlet like a soldier" to a high platform accompanied by the rites of a military funeral, "For he was likely, had he been put on,/To have proved most royal." As the soldiers bear Hamlet upward to the sounds of cannons, the tragedy comes to a fitting end.

CONCLUDING COMMENT

Horatio has spoken of two kinds of deaths, "of accidental judgments, casual slaughters," on the one hand, and, on the other, "of deaths put on by cunning and forced cause,/And, in this upshot, purposes mistook/Fall'n on th' inventors' heads." The first type characterizes Hamlet, whose killings have all been accidental or casual. The second type characterizes the "deep plots" of Claudius and Laertes, who have tried to shape their ends directly with the ironic result of punishing themselves and those most dear. In either case we may equally see the hand of the "divinity that shapes our ends." Hamlet has allowed Providence to work itself out through him; Claudius and Laertes have tried to shape their own destinies and for this are punished. The distinction between them, however, raises Hamlet above Claudius and all his accomplices, whatever the extent of their complicity.

But if Hamlet deserves our admiration for his final "readiness" to accept and further the will of heaven, his life also stands forfeit for the bloody course he has traveled to this end. It is this tension between earthly defeat and spiritual redemption which makes Hamlet's death truly tragic. For at the very moment when he has finally achieved a full "readiness" for a noble life, when "he was likely, had he been put on,/To have proved most royal," his life is over. Though we mourn the tragic waste of his potential, we must also glory that he has won a victory in defeat, seeing with Hamlet that "the readiness is all."

CHARACTER ANALYSES

HAMLET

Hamlet dares us to "pluck out the heart of my mystery." This mystery marks the essence of Hamlet's character. Ophelia tells us that before the events of the play Hamlet was a model courtier, soldier, and scholar, "The glass of fashion and the mould of form,/Th' observed of all observers." With the death of his father and the hasty, incestuous remarriage of his mother to his uncle, however, Hamlet is thrown into a suicidal frame of mind in which "the uses of this world" seem to him "weary, stale, flat, and unprofitable." Though his faith in the value of life has been destroyed by this double confrontation with death and human infidelity, he feels impotent to effect any change in this new reality: "It is not, nor it cannot come to good./But break my heart, for I must hold my tongue." All he can do in this frustrated state is to lash out with bitter satire at the evils he sees and then relapse into suicidal melancholy.

It is in this state that he meets the equally mysterious figure of his father's Ghost with its supernatural revelations of murder and adultery and its injunction upon Hamlet to revenge his father's murder. While this command gives purpose and direction to Hamlet's hitherto frustrated impulse toward scourging reform, it also serves to further unsettle his already disturbed reason. When two months later he forces his way into Ophelia's room, he looks "As if he had been loosed out of hell/To speak of horrors." Whether or not the Ghost was actually a devil, its effect upon Hamlet has been diabolic.

In the two months after his meeting with the Ghost, he puzzles the court with his assumed madness but does nothing concrete to further his revenge. His inability to either accept the goodness of life or act to destroy its evils now begins to trouble him as much as his outward hysteria and depression does the court. He first condemns his apparent lack of concentration on his revenge as the sign of a base, cowardly nature. The players' arrival, however, gives him an idea for testing the Ghost's truth and Claudius' guilt. Rationalizing his inactivity as an effect of his doubt about the Ghost's nature, he plans to have the players perform a play which reproduces Claudius' crime and observe Claudius' reaction to it, thereby dispelling his own doubts as to the proper course of his action. Having momentarily silenced his shame at his inaction, however, he immediately relapses into his former state; he meditates upon suicide and then lashes out with satiric cruelty at Ophelia.

The play successfully reveals Claudius' guilt to Hamlet, and Hamlet reacts to this proof with wild glee. His old friends Rosencrantz and Guildenstern, who had returned to Elsinore to help further Claudius' investigation into Hamlet's disorder and had thereby alienated Hamlet's affections, enter with a message from Hamlet's mother that she wishes to see him immediately. Hamlet treats them contemptuously before returning his answer that he will go to his mother. His coming visit with his mother inspires him with a murderous rage appropriate to the hellish time of night. Once more in the power of hell, he accidentally comes upon the praying figure of Claudius but does not take this opportunity for revenge because of the devilish rationalization that such revenge would not damn Claudius' soul. But the truth seems to be that Hamlet's murderous rage is misdirected at his mother rather than at Claudius, even though Hamlet is now fully convinced of his guilt. Coming to his mother's room with the intent to punish her with verbal daggers for her unfaithfulness, her unwilling-ness to listen to him releases his murderous impulse against her. In a moment of temporary insanity he manages to exer-cise enough control to deflect the blow designed for her to the direction of an unexpected sound, killing Polonius. In the ensuing scene he all but forgets Polonius' body in his urgency to arouse his mother's guilt for her treatment of his father and injury to his own trust.

This fact, together with his obsessed preoccupation with his mother's sexual life, may provide a clue to the "mystery" of Hamlet. Hamlet had admitted to Ophelia that women's sensual falseness "hath made me mad." Once he is reconciled to his mother, the whole of reality appears to him in a different light.

Where before his will was "most incorrect to heaven," the "Everlasting" seeming to be the creator of sterile farces and imposer of harsh laws, he now accepts heaven's purposes and allies himself with them as heaven's "scourge and minister." Seeing the hand of heaven in his accidental slaying of Polonius as well as in the exile to England which will result from it, he is able to accept this turn of events with new confidence in his ultimate success.

Hamlet's change in attitude begun in his mother's room continues to develop while on shipboard and is responsible for his actions there. Inspired by his restlessness, he forges a new commission which substitutes for his death the deaths of Rosencrantz and Guildenstern and manages to free himself from the Danish ship. In all of this he sees "heaven ordinant" and this teaches him that "There's a divinity that shapes our ends,/Rough-hew them how we will." Recognizing by this that humanly conceived plots are doomed to fail, he places himself completely in the hands of Providence.

His belief in the providential control of all events is justified by the outcome. Laertes establishes Claudius' responsibility for Hamlet's death and the death of his mother and Hamlet is able to execute Claudius for these crimes alone. Hamlet has transcended his earlier damnable intention of premeditated revenge in a spontaneous act of just repayment for the loss of his own life. Recognizing that "the readiness is all," Hamlet has finally achieved this readiness to endure both life and death. His final actions are his most life affirming, his restraining of Horatio from committing suicide and his concern for the continuing welfare of Denmark. The tragedy of his death is that it comes at the moment when "he was likely, had he been put on,/To have proved most royal." Destroyed and redeemed by the same brilliance of perception, Hamlet's spirit has undergone a tragic development from the self-destructive negation of life and of heaven's purposes to a new affirmation of the providential sanctity of life, and it is this final "readiness" which redeems him.

CLAUDIUS

At the beginning of the play, Claudius has achieved his heart's desire and is fully confident of his ability to preserve his position. If it cost him any pain to commit adultery with his brother's wife and then kill him, this cost is now forgotten in the happy possession of his crown and beloved Queen. Now that he has his throne and Queen he wants only peace to enjoy them. In an admirable diplomatic move, he averts war with Norway. In his more personal diplomacy, he wins the support of the chief counselors of state for all of his plans and tries most earnestly to win Hamlet's goodwill by requesting that he remain in Denmark to enjoy his royal favor. He believes in making the best of a difficult situation and preaches such acceptance to Hamlet.

But if Hamlet was still in conspicuous mourning two months after his father's death and appeared to grudge Claudius his throne and marriage, in four months time his behavior has become dangerously provocative. Anxious to overcome this single impediment to his security and the smooth functioning of his state, Claudius sets spies on Hamlet to try to understand what is troubling him. Rosencrantz and Guildenstern can tell him nothing, but the scene he witnesses between Hamlet and Ophelia, in which Hamlet seemed to threaten his life, convinces him that he must act immediately to protect himself, and he decides to do this by sending Hamlet off to England for a time.

Though he has controlled himself very well up until this time,

Claudius' composure breaks down at the play. Hamlet has aroused Claudius' guilt. Although he preaches the acceptance of his evil as the will of heaven, he was unable to accept the heavenly dispensation which gave his brother everything that he desired and so he made himself the god of his own universe and celebrated his power with the earthly thunder of cannons.

Hamlet's insane murder of Polonius, however, puts an end to Claudius' hesitation. He can no longer deny Hamlet's extreme danger to him and self-preservation overrides the objections of his conscience and his loving concern for Gertrude's peace of mind. But as his conscience was strong enough to arouse his guilt but not sufficiently powerful to cause him to forego his life and happiness, so now it does not prevent him from planning Hamlet's murder but makes him too squeamish to perform it himself. He plots to convert Hamlet's exile into his death, though he does not stop to consider how he will later answer for this death. When this plot fails, he immediately plans another, this time using Laertes instead of the King of England as his instrument. Again the plot is conceived in too desperate a state to really mark its consequences, and this time its failure is so awful that it involves the accidental death of his beloved wife and his own final end.

Relying upon his continuing ability to shape his destiny, Claudius piles misconceived plot upon plot in a desperate attempt to preserve his ill-gotten gains. Though he keeps his head when Laertes threatens his throne and, more fearfully, when Gertrude drinks the poison he had prepared for Hamlet, he is so concerned to preserve his life that he has forgotten his soul. He has missed the opportunity of repenting his former sins and dies with an unprepared soul.

GERTRUDE
The beloved wife and mother of the play's "mighty opposites" has no mind of her own and is pulled by whatever force is most powerfully directed at her at any moment. By

temperament she turns to the sunny side of life and cannot bear to face any pain or conflict.

Hamlet's refusal to forget his father's death or to forgive his mother's hasty and incestuous remarriage is the only blot on her happiness. It continues to remind her of the continuing difficulties of her position which she had naively hoped would be ended by her marriage. If she could only get Hamlet to accept her new husband as his new father, she could completely bury the past in the happy present. She therefore begs him to remain at Elsinore so that this reconciliation can take place. But as she watches her beloved and remarkable son become more and more deranged with the passing months, her happiness becomes blighted. She hopes that Rosencrantz and Guildenstern will be able to bring him out of his depression. Then she snatches at the possibility that Hamlet's disturbance might actually be caused by his love for Ophelia rather than her own behavior and hopes that Ophelia will be able to cure him. Her spirits rise for a moment when she sees Hamlet's excited involvement with the play and his attentions to Ophelia, but then they immediately drop as Claudius rises from the performance in anguish.

When Ophelia goes mad, Gertrude wishes to avoid the painful sight of her as much as she had earlier wished to avoid looking into her own soul. Gertrude sees Ophelia's mental breakdown as further proof of the continuing evil caused by her unthinking behavior, and this chain of evil effects seems to bode some great catastrophe. Though deeply grieved by Ophelia's death, she tries, nonetheless, to explain it to herself and to Laertes in the least damaging way. But her sorrow at Ophelia's funeral is accentuated by the madness her son displays there.

She is delighted when Hamlet appears at the fencing match in such a reasonable frame of mind. Not only does Laertes appear to accept Hamlet's offer of love, but Hamlet's own willingness to fight as Claudius' champion seems to promise her their reconciliation as well. If Laertes were reconciled to Hamlet and Hamlet to Claudius, all the horror of her guilt and Ophelia's death might yet be forgotten and she might still be granted the happiness that she had thought Ophelia's marriage to Claudius would bring her. In this blind hope of future happiness, her son's gentlemanly behavior and excellence of fencing so intoxicate her that she joins fully into the event, coming forward to wipe her dear boy's brow and insisting upon toasting his coming victory.

As she has ever evaded the prospect of anything painful in the hope of achieving happiness, so it is fitting that this flaw should prove her destruction. Only as she feels the poison creeping over her and hears her husband lie about her condition to save himself does she face reality. Only then does she begin to understand Hamlet's objections to Claudius and recognize that Claudius has poisoned her whole life as now he has her body. Trying too late to protect her "dear Hamlet," she dies the miserable victim of her sentimental and deluded hope for happiness.

POLONIUS

The Lord Chamberlain and chief courtier at Elsinore, Polonius appears to have been flattered into giving his support to Claudius. But Claudius' flattery is nothing to Polonius' self-flattery. He detains Laertes' departure with stale advice about proper behavior. Upon learning of his daughter Ophelia's involvement with Hamlet, he immediately decides that Hamlet's intentions must be dishonorable and forbids his innocent daughter from seeing him again. Judging both Hamlet and Laertes by his own youthful indulgences, he not only prejudges Hamlet's interest in his daughter but sends his servant, Reynaldo, to spy upon Laertes in Paris. He is at his height as he explains the refinements of spying to Reynaldo and cares nothing that in his concern to find out the worst about his son he may actually be hurting Laertes' reputation.

Like a dutiful daughter, Ophelia comes immediately to her father to report Hamlet's strange behavior upon forcing himself into her room. As quickly as he had assumed Hamlet's dishonorable intentions, so now he decides that it was true love and that Ophelia's rejection of him has driven him mad. He admits that his earlier orders to Ophelia were lacking in sound judgment but sets his authoritarian presumption down to the natural effects of age. Seeing in Ophelia's relationship to Hamlet a way to further endear himself to the King and perhaps offset any other adverse effects his age may have had against him, he immediately takes his trembling daughter off to the King.

Having interested the King and Queen in his theory of Hamlet's madness, Polonius further plans to prostitute his daughter's modesty to gain the King's favor by suggesting that a meeting be arranged between his daughter and Hamlet which the King and he would spy upon. He tries to investigate Hamlet himself, though Hamlet only makes fun of him in the most contemptuous way. All his concern is now to maintain his privileged position at court as Chief Counselor to the King.

Polonius suggests a new spying plan to Claudius which might vindicate his own theory or reveal a new solution to their dilemmas. But the overanxious, presumptuous, and self-deluding fool has blundered again. Concerned only with his own self-importance and incapable of understanding Hamlet, Polonius precipitates a situation which ends with his own accidental death. Hamlet speaks the most fitting closing description of him when he says: "Thou wretched, rash, intruding fool, farewell!" But if Polonius' efforts on behalf of his children have been as damaging to them as they have been on his own behalf, their effects live on beyond him. Lost without the father upon whom she had obediently depended for her every thought and act, Ophelia loses her mind and meets her death. The false and outward sense of honor Polonius has implanted in Laertes causes him to try to revenge his father's death in a most underhanded way and leads to his own death as well. As he is as poor a counselor to himself as he was to others, we must finally agree with Hamlet: "Indeed, this counsellor/Is now most still, most secret, and most grave,/Who was in life a foolish prating knave."

OPHELIA

"Pretty Ophelia," as Claudius calls her, is the most innocent victim of Hamlet's revenge. Attracted by her sweet beauty, Hamlet had fallen in love with her. She had "sucked the honey of his music vows" and returned his affection. But when her father had challenged the honor of Hamlet's intentions, Ophelia could only reply: "I do not know, my lord, what I should think." Used to relying upon her father's direction and brought up to be obedient, she can only accept her father's belief, seconded by that of her brother, that Hamlet's "holy vows" of love were simply designed for her seduction and obey her father's orders not to permit Hamlet to see her again.

When his mother's hasty remarriage had led Hamlet to the disillusioned view that "frailty, thy name is woman," Ophelia's affection might yet have restored his spirit. But her unexplained refusal to see him soon after his mother's remarriage completes Hamlet's disillusionment with women. The Ghost's revelation that his mother had not only dishonored his father's memory but also their marriage by her adultery with Claudius festers in his mind for two months until he finally forces his way into Ophelia's room to look upon her again. Searching her innocent face for some sign of loving truth that might restore his faith in her and, through her, in womankind and in love, he takes her mute terror for a further sign of her guilt and sees her as but another false Gertrude.

Ophelia is still too much under her father's influence to question his wisdom or authority, and she has no mind of her own to understand how she has made her lover suffer. After a hopeful beginning, Ophelia ruins her chances by the foolish strategy of accusing Hamlet of rejecting her. This only enrages him against her duplicity and he cruelly denies ever having loved or given her anything. As his savage attack proceeds, Ophelia is again convinced of his madness and her hopes sink to despairing prayers to heaven to restore him. As she sees what has happened to her noble lover and to her earlier hopes for their love, she is overcome by her woe. At the play that evening he comes to sit by her, but whatever joy this might have given her is blasted by the disrespectful and vulgar way that he jokes with her. No longer addressing her "with love/In honorable fashion," he treats her like a whore. When that night her father is mysteriously killed and then obscurely buried in great haste it is too much for her. Abused by her lover, bereft of her father's protection, alone, and overcome by the sense of her dishonor and that of her father, she loses control of her mind.

LAERTES

Laertes is a young man whose good instincts have been somewhat obscured by the concern with superficial appearances which he has learned from his father, Polonius. After a brief appearance at court to beg Claudius' leave to return to Paris, we see him again pompously lecturing his sister Ophelia about men's hypocritical ways and warning her to protect her chastity against "Hamlet, and the trifling of his favor." With some apparent knowledge of her brother's ways, she replies that he should not preach strictness to her while himself acting like a "reckless libertine." Like his father, Laertes apparently preaches a morality he does not practice and fully believes in a double standard of behavior for the sexes.

When he learns of his father's unexplained death and obscure funeral, Laertes' sense of honor is touched to the quick. Since honor demands that he revenge his father's death, he returns to Denmark, gathers a rabble mob together, and storms the castle, demanding that the King answer for his father's death. As unconcerned for the order of society as he is for his own salvation, he would rather "dare damnation" than leave his father's honor and his own besmirched. Though the sight of his sister's madness brings him to a moment of true grief, he is still primarily enraged by his father's "obscure funeral—/No trophy, sword, nor hatchment o'er his bones,/No noble rite nor formal ostentation."

When Claudius explains Hamlet's responsibility for Polonius' death and his own reasons for covering up this fact, Laertes is satisfied to work with Claudius to achieve his revenge against Hamlet. If there was any chance of his renouncing such a dishonorable plan, Hamlet's behavior at his sister's funeral puts a quick end to this. Though his grief may take an ostentatious form, Hamlet's challenge to his right to grieve, his fight with him in the very grave and then his insulting remarks upon leaving only re-enforce Laertes' resolution. Still, there was an opportunity during the scene for Laertes to achieve his revenge in the spirit of true honor. When Hamlet responds to Laertes' curses by offering him a duel to the death, Laertes might have accepted this offer and tried to achieve his revenge in a fair manner. But Hamlet's self-righteous behavior so outrages Laertes that his sense of honor becomes completely warped by his hatred for Hamlet and he cannot afford to take his chances with him.

At the start of the fencing match, Hamlet excuses his behavior at the funeral and his accidental slaying of Polonius on the grounds of his madness and asks for Laertes' pardon. Laertes has an opportunity to renounce his plan of revenge, but he is so concerned about his formal and outward "terms of honor" that he cannot permit his natural feelings to rule his will. In this concern for outward honor he further dishonors himself by the false statement that he will act honorably with Hamlet. Saying that "I do receive your offered love like love,/And will not wrong it," he goes and chooses the lethally sharp and poisoned weapon.

When Hamlet begins to taunt him for his poor performance, it is too much for Laertes' pride. Playing as best he can, he is astonished to find that he can only bring Hamlet to a draw. His vengeance now enraged by jealousy at Hamlet's fine sportsmanship and true gentlemanly bearing, he lunges at Hamlet after the close of the formal bout and manages to wound him. When, by his wound, Hamlet realizes Laertes' false practice, he returns to the fight with such power that he captures Laertes' foil and wounds him fatally with it.

Had Laertes acted upon the honorable promptings of his conscience, he would have avoided his own death and, by allying himself with Hamlet, would have won the gratitude of the future King. Laertes' false sense of honor and pride override his better instincts to the fatal harm of both. Recognizing his dishonor too late and admitting that he is "justly killed with mine own treachery," Laertes finally rises to the true honor of admitting his fault to Hamlet, informing him of Claudius' designs, and then, in a tragically belated reconciliation with Hamlet, offering him an exchange of forgiveness. But if his rise to true honor finally redeems him in our eyes, his false honor has destroyed his life.

ROSENCRANTZ AND GUILDENSTERN

Shakespeare's doubling of the type of courtier represented by both Rosencrantz and Guildenstern shows that tragic lack of individuality which this type possesses. They so revere their King that they are willing "to lay our service freely at your feet,/To be commanded." Claudius' employment of them seems perfectly consistent with their honor.

Though Rosencrantz and Guildenstern are not conscious criminals, since they are unaware of the criminal designs of the King they obey, the fact that "they did make love to this employment" without any scrutiny into the King's purposes does condemn them as unthinking accomplices. If as model courtiers they feel they have nothing on their consciences, their lack of individual integrity and total dependence upon the King doom them to the fate of the King to whom they are thus "mortised and adjoined."

HORATIO

Horatio returns to Elsinore from Wittenburg for the funeral of Hamlet's father and remains to become Hamlet's one true friend. When Marcellus brings this university scholar to witness the sight of the Ghost, he reports this event not to Claudius but to Hamlet. Hamlet swears Horatio to keep the knowledge of the Ghost and of Hamlet's further purposes confidential, and he never breaks this confidence.

During the next two months Horatio's integrity and emotional reserve so win Hamlet's admiration that he fully takes him to his heart. Here is a friend whose integrity he can fully trust and whose Stoic reserve acts to calm his own passionate response to evil. He takes Horatio fully into his confidence about the disclosures of the Ghost and about his further plan to test Claudius through the performance of a play. When Hamlet reacts to Claudius' breakdown with hysterical glee, Horatio quietly calms him down so that they can discuss the implications of Claudius' reaction more sanely.

Hamlet had earlier praised Horatio as one "whose blood and judgment are so well commingled." Upon returning to Denmark, he immediately sends for Horatio as he longs to confide the new horrors of his trip to him and gain his judicial acceptance for his further plans.

As Horatio tries to protect Hamlet when he is dying, Hamlet protects his friend from following him through suicide. This shows how fully "mortised and adjoined" Horatio feels toward Hamlet. However much he may have questioned Hamlet's reactions and behavior, he has fully committed himself to Hamlet's fate and only permits himself to live so that he may justify Hamlet's life and death. When Hamlet dies,

Horatio speaks the eulogy over him, commending his "noble heart" and his soul to heaven. With his death, Horatio takes control of events, arranges for the funerals, and hands over the kingdom, in accordance with Hamlet's wishes, to Fortinbras.

FORTINBRAS

Perhaps the greatest irony in this ironic play is Fortinbras' inheritance of the Danish kingdom. For Fortinbras is the son of the Norwegian King whose defeat was Hamlet's father's greatest victory. If Hamlet's revenge was supposed to vindicate his father's honor, the suicidal way in which he proceeded with this revenge resulted in completely burying his father's glory with his empire.

Having proven his honor in the successful exploit against Poland, Fortinbras picks the plum of Denmark without any effort. By not attacking Denmark, the Danish crown has fallen into his lap. Here we may again detect the ironic hand of Providence.

THE GHOST

Whether it be the "honest Ghost" of Hamlet's father come from Purgatory or a diabolic or angelic agent of Providence is never made completely clear. This ambiguity reinforces the central mystery of the play. Although Providence accomplishes Claudius' destruction, which the Ghost's had demanded of Hamlet, the Ghost's demands also unsettle Hamlet. Such results indicate the morally questionable nature of the Ghost's demands. The Ghost's influence upon Hamlet has been powerful enough to wrench Hamlet's spirit out of its normal frame so that he destroys himself in the destruction of his enemies.

COMMENTARY ON THE CRITICISM

BRIEF NOTE ON THE CRITICISM

Hamlet's mysterious delay in fulfilling his revenge has led to much critical speculation about the so-called "problem of Hamlet." From Goethe and Coleridge to Freud and his disciples, many people have probed Hamlet's character. More recently, this question has been placed in the larger context of the whole play's mysterious quality. Hamlet's character now points to the deeper mystery of reality which is concentrated in the mysterious figure of the Ghost and the ironic workings of Providence. *Hamlet* has come to be viewed not simply as the psychological tragedy of its hero but as profound religious drama which attempts to explore as well the cosmic mysteries of existence.

KEY POINTS IN THE CRITICISM

Major critics have raised certain central questions about the play:

1. A primary question is whether this celebrated tragedy is a perfect work of art.

2. The most consistently raised question concerns Hamlet. Is he a healthy Renaissance prince, a depraved egomaniac, or an essentially noble and sensitive hero whose spirit has been disturbed by the task of revenge imposed upon him? If the latter is true, what has so disturbed him as to seriously delay the prosecution of his revenge? Is it a weak will, the product of over-intellectualizing, the result of melancholy, or an Oedipus Complex?

3. How important is Hamlet's character to the structure of the play as a whole? Does the mystery of Hamlet's disturbance point to a deeper mystery at the heart of the play? Is this mystery a fault or a virtue of the design? What is the relationship of the Ghost to this mystery? Is *Hamlet* a religious drama? These and their related questions will be discussed in the following historical survey of the outstanding criticism on *Hamlet*.

The first major critical treatment of *Hamlet* came from Dr. Samuel Johnson in 1765. Dr. Johnson commented on Hamlet's moral nature. He noted that Hamlet treats Ophelia with "wanton cruelty" and that the speech made over the praying figure of Claudius "in which Hamlet, represented as a virtuous character, is not content with taking blood for blood, but contrives damnation for the man that he would punish, is too horrible to be read or to be uttered."

The major historical tradition accepts Hamlet as an example of Aristotle's model tragic hero, one who is generally better than the average but is brought down by a flaw in his character. The first major proponent of this position was Johann Wolfgang von Goethe in his *Wilhelm Meister's Apprenticeship,* written in 1796: "Shakespeare sought to depict a great deed laid upon a soul unequal to the performance of it. . . . A beautiful, pure, noble and most moral nature, without the strength of nerve which forms a hero, sinks beneath a burden which it can neither bear nor throw off; every duty is holy to him—this is too hard. The impossible is required of him—not the impossible in itself, but the impossible to him. How he winds, turns, agonizes, advances, and recoils, ever reminded, ever reminding himself, and at last almost loses his purpose from his thoughts, without ever again recovering his peace of mind." Goethe's noble but weak-willed hero has had long critical and theatrical popularity.

A. C. Bradley's important essay on *Hamlet in Shakespearean Tragedy,* written in 1904, represents both the critique and culmination of romantic criticism. Bradley's key to Hamlet's character is a pathological state of melancholy: "The direct cause [of Hamlet's delay] was a state of mind quite abnormal and induced by special circumstances—a state of profound melancholy." Hamlet's reflectiveness doubtless played a certain part in the production of that melancholy, and was thus one indirect contributory cause of his irresolution. The melancholy, once established, displayed, as one of its symptoms, an excessive reflection on the required deed. Bradley shows that melancholy "accounts for Hamlet's energy as well as for his lassitude." He also attributes to Hamlet's melancholy those "painful features of his character" which Johnson had first noted. Bradley judges Hamlet's basic and original character as being "by temperament . . . inclined to nervous instability," as having both "an exquisite sensibility, to which we may give the name 'moral,' and intellectual genius." As such, he feels that "Hamlet deserves the title 'tragedy of moral idealism' . . ." Although he considers the psychological impediment greater than the intellectual, he also feels that it is Hamlet's genius which raises his story from the pathological to the tragic and makes Hamlet "the symbol of a tragic mystery inherent in human nature."

In 1919, T. S. Eliot published "Hamlet and His Problems." Eliot said that *Hamlet* represents an imperfect fusion of old crude material with new, creating "an artistic failure." Eliot continues: "Hamlet (the man) is dominated by an emotion which is inexpressible, because it is in excess of the facts as they appear. . . . We should have to understand things which Shakespeare did not understand himself."

In 1935, John Dover Wilson published *What Happens in Hamlet*. Wilson's primary concern is to make sense of the plot. He also focuses our attention on the multiple investigations which take up most of the action in the second and third acts. The mystery first suggested by the Ghost and later accentuated through the cross investigations of Hamlet, Cladius, and Polonius is finally seen to extend to the character of Hamlet, himself: "In fine, we were never intended to reach the heart of the mystery. That it has a heart is an illusion; the mystery itself is an illusion; Hamlet is an illusion. The secret that lies behind it all is not Hamlet's, but Shakespeare's: the technical devices he employed to create this supreme illusion of a great and mysterious character. . ." In seeing the sense of mystery as product of Shakespeare's consummate design, Wilson has set the line for much of the criticism which has followed.

In 1960, critic Bernard Grebanier claimed that Hamlet did not procrastinate, was not unduly disturbed, and went about his revenge as efficiently as circumstances permitted. In *The Heart of Hamlet*, Grebanier makes the most extended argument for a "healthy" Hamlet: "To know how Hamlet feels about life we must watch not what he says about it so much as what he does living it. Look at him in this way, and you will find him not melancholy, not complex-ridden, not pessimistic, not even disillusioned basically—but a healthy, vigorous man, much in love with life, who, given the slightest opportunity, is happy, cheerful, companionable, and kind." Grebanier concludes: "Shakespeare's *Hamlet,* then, is not a play about a man who procrastinates or a man who feigns madness. Neither appears in the work. . . .

> Hamlet falls not because he is too timid, too sensitive, too thoughtful, or too scrupulous, but because he is too rash, too overweening, too heedless.

See the Bibliography for other critical interpretations.

ESSAY QUESTIONS AND ANSWERS

QUESTION
Does Hamlet procrastinate in prosecuting his revenge?

ANSWER
Yes, Hamlet does procrastinate in prosecuting his revenge. Although Hamlet had said that he would be "swift" and "sweep to my revenge," in the "rogue and peasant slave" soliloquy, Hamlet admits that he has been "unpregnant of my cause" and wonders whether he is a "coward." It is only after he is filled with disgust with himself for his long delay that he seeks confirmation of Claudius' guilt. However, he rationalizes this away with the argument that Claudius' soul might escape eternal damnation. En route to his exile in England, Hamlet refers to his "dull revenge" in the important soliloquy in which he admits: "I do not know/Why yet I live to say 'This thing's to do';/Sith I have cause and will and strength and means/To do't." And he now vows, in opposition to his attitude of the past two months: "O! from this time forth,/My thoughts be bloody, or be nothing worth!"

QUESTION
If Hamlet does procrastinate, what is the reason for his delay?

ANSWER
Hamlet's overly intellectual mind inhibited him from taking any decisive action. Hamlet gives some support to this view in two soliloquies. In the "to be or not to be" soliloquy, Hamlet concludes: "Thus conscience [consciousness] does make cowards of us all;/And thus the native hue of resolution/Is sicklied o'er with the pale cast of thought." In the soliloquy en route to exile, Hamlet wonders whether the delay in his revenge is due to "some craven scruple/Of thinking too precisely on the event,/A thought, which, quarter'd, hath but one part wisdom, and ever three parts coward."

While there is no question that Hamlet has a brilliant mind and devotes much time to thinking about his problems, he tends to rationalize his procrastination. Thus, having considered the hypothesis that his delay is due to "thinking too precisely on the event," he immediately continues, "I do not know/why yet I live to say 'This thing's to do,'" thereby completely rejecting this possible explanation.

QUESTION

In what sense is Hamlet the hero and Claudius the villain of the play?

ANSWER

Claudius is the true villain and Hamlet the hero in the spiritual world of Shakespeare's play. To Shakespeare, that which distinguishes the hero from the villain is the perception of humanity's necessary dependence on the divine will. Though Claudius had counseled Hamlet that his refusal to accept the death of his father "shows a will most incorrect to heaven," he had himself been guilty of the same inability to accept the divine dispensation that gave his brother the crown and woman he loved. Instead, he had plotted to shape his own destiny by first murdering his brother and then planning Hamlet's death. Claudius had made himself the god of his own universe. When all his attempts to shape his ends backfire, he dies spiritually deluded and unready.

Hamlet also begins in a state of spiritual alienation from God's purposes, unable to accept God's creation while prevented by His law from committing suicide. But after murdering Polonius in a moment of insanity, he suddenly understands his relationship to the divine in a new light: "heaven hath pleas'd it so,/To punish me with this, and this with me,/That I must be their scourge and minister." Where before he had felt alienated from the divine will, he now feels himself to be in harmony with it and sees himself as a vessel for the fulfillment of Providence. He perceives this new insight even more deeply after he seals the fate of his old school fellows Rosencrantz and Guildenstern. In a most important speech in which he praises his rashness, he explains:

> And prais'd be rashness for it—let us know/Our indis-cretion sometimes serves us well/When our deep plots do pall, and that should learn us/There's a divinity that shapes our ends,/Rough-hew them how we will—

Although Hamlet had returned without taking any precautions for his safety or making any plans for Claudius' death, the duel with Laertes, in which both Hamlet and Laertes are mortally wounded and the Queen poisoned, leads to Laertes' confession of Claudius' guilt. This, in turn, permits Hamlet to execute Claudius judicially. Though he is himself mortally punished for his divine ministry, he has performed divine will through his complete dependence upon Providence. He dies believing that "the readiness is all," having finally achieved the ability to accept both life and death. His last acts, restraining Horatio from suicide and voting Fortinbras the new King, are his most life-affirming. Where Claudius is unready for death and has damned himself by the piling up of evil plots to shape his ends, Hamlet has most nobly won his salvation.

QUESTION
Why does the tragic conflict of Hamlet and Claudius leave so many other deaths in its wake?

ANSWER
In the world of tragedy, the scourging of evil often involves a wrenching of natural order. In the process, many of those who have attached themselves to the original wrongdoer are destroyed.

The simplest examples of this process are Rosencrantz and Guildenstern. As model courtiers, they obey the King's orders without presuming to examine their nature. When this involves them in carrying Claudius' orders for Hamlet's execution, they become criminal accomplices of a criminal King and are liable to the punishment which Hamlet metes out to them.

A more complex example is Polonius. A presumptuous fool, Polonius is anxious to prove his worth through his aptitude for spying. Having arranged one unsuccessful spying incident in which he and Claudius watched a meeting between Hamlet and Ophelia, he plans another confrontation between Hamlet and Gertrude. His anxiety to prove his worth is also joined to a failing perception of human motivation, especially of one so complex as Hamlet. As he first misjudged Hamlet's intentions toward his daughter, so now he fatally misjudges the passionate involvement of Hamlet with his mother's sins, and the murderous outburst to which their meeting soon leads results in his own death.

BIBLIOGRAPHY

EARLIER CRITICISM
Coleridge, Samuel Taylor. *Coleridge's Shakespearean Criticism.* Thomas Middleton Raysor, ed. Cambridge: Harvard University Press, 1930.

Goethe, Johann Wolfgang von. *Wilhelm Meister's Apprenticeship* (1796), trans. Thomas Carlyle (1824). London: Chapman and Hall Ltd., n.d. (Vol. I, Book IV, Chapter XIII).

Johnson, Samuel. *Johnson on Shakespeare: Essays and Notes Selected and Set Forth with an Introduction by Walter Raleigh.* London: Oxford University Press, 1908.

TWENTIETH CENTURY CRITICISM
Berkhoff, Steven. *I Am Hamlet.* New York: Grove Weidenfeld, 1990.

Bradley, A. C. *Shakespearean Tragedy.* New York: Meridian Books, 1955. (1904)

Burdett, Lois. *A Child's Portrait of Shakespeare.* Buffalo, New York: Firefly Press, 1995.

Calderwood, James L. *To Be or Not to Be: Negation and Metadrama in Hamlet.* New York: Columbia University Press, 1983.

Charney, Maurice. *Hamlet's Fictions.* New York: Routledge, 1988.

Cohen, Michael. *Hamlet in My Mind's Eye.* Athens, Georgia: University of Georgia Press, 1989.

Critical Essays on Shakespeare's Hamlet. New York: G. K. Hall, 1995.

Eliot, T. S. "Hamlet and His Problems" (1919), in *Selected Essays: 1917-1932*. New York: Harcourt, Brace and Company, 1932.

Fraser, Russell A. *Shakespeare, the Later Years*. New York: Columbia University Press, 1992.

Frye, Roland. *Shakespeare: The Art of the Dramatist*. Boston: Allen and Unwin, 1982.

Grebanier, Bernard. *The Heart of Hamlet: The Play Shakespeare Wrote*. New York: Thomas Y. Crowell Company, 1960.

Hamlet. New York: Chelsea House, 1990.

Hamlet: Critical Essays. New York: Garland Publishers, 1986.

Hattaway, Michael. *Hamlet*. Atlantic Highlands, NJ: Humanities Press International, 1987.

Johnson, Robert A. *Transformation: Understanding the Three Levels of Masculine Consciousness*, 1991.

Kerrigan, William. *Hamlet's Perfection*. Baltimore: Johns Hopkins University Press, 1994.

King, Walter. *Hamlet's Search for Meaning*. Athens: University of Georgia Press, 1982.

Levi, Peter. *The Life and Times of William Shakespeare*. New York: Holt, 1995.

Martin, Christopher. *Shakespeare*. Vero Beach, Florida: Rourke Enterprises, 1988.

Rosenberg, Marvin. *The Masks of Hamlet*. Newark: University of Delaware Press, 1992.

Schmidgall, Gary. *Shakespeare and Opera.* New York: Oxford University Press, 1990.

Schoenbaum, Samuel. *Shakespeare: His Life, His English, His Theatre.* New York: Signet Classic, 1990.

Trewin, J.C. *Five and Eighty Hamlets.* New York: New Amsterdam, 1989.

Watts, Cedric. *Hamlet.* Boston: Twayne Publishers, 1988.

Wells, Stanley. *Shakespeare: A Life in Drama.* New York: W. W. Norton, 1995.

William Shakespeare's Hamlet. New York: Chelsea House Publishers, 1996.

Wilson, John Dover. *What Happens in Hamlet.* Cambridge: The University Press, 1962. (1935)

Wood, Robert. *Some Necessary Questions of the Play: A Stage-Centered Analysis of Shakespeare's Hamlet.* 1994.

NOTES

NOTES

NOTES

NOTES

NOTES

NOTES

NOTES

NOTES

NOTES

NOTES